GW00659720

SAFE AS HOUSES

Wimbledon at War
1939-1945
THIRD EDITION

The Story of a London Suburb

Norman Plastow MBE FRIBA

Published by The Wimbledon Society
a registered charity, No. 269478
22 Ridgway, Wimbledon

© Norman Plastow 2010

Printed by Intype Libra Ltd, Wimbledon

3rd Edition

ISBN 978-0-9511378-8-8

CONTENTS

ILUSTRATIONS

INTRODUCTION

The first battle of Wimbledon is said to have taken place in AD 568 when the leader of the West Saxons fought against the King of Kent and two Ealdormen were killed. We know very little about that battle because few records were kept at that time. What is surprising, however, is that the second battle of Wimbledon, in which one hundred and fifty people were killed, over a thousand injured and nearly fourteen thousand houses were damaged or destroyed, was never officially recorded.

The account that follows is the story of a typical suburb of London during the period 1939-1945. Wimbledon did not suffer the same devastation as some inner London Boroughs, nor was it the most heavily bombed but it was one of the first London suburbs to be attacked and during the flying bomb raids of 1944 it was said to hold the title of being 'The hottest of the suburbs in which civilised people were attempting to remain alive'. The number of incidents recorded in the following pages and shown on the incident map at the end of this book may surprise even those who lived through these years.

Many records have been lost or destroyed but in the case of Wimbledon it has been possible to reconstruct the history of the war years due to the personal initiative of certain people who managed to preserve documentary evidence. The original incident map from the wall of the Control Room in Wimbledon Town Hall was thrown away when the new London Borough of Merton was formed but was salvaged from a skip by local historian Miss Evelyn Jowett. Lt.Cdr. W.R.C. Varlow, who took over the civil defence services after the war, found the last complete set of incident reports at the back of a filing cabinet in the Mayor's office and many people have helped with diaries, photographs and personal recollections. I should like to thank them all.

Norman Plastow

Evacuees at Wimbledon Station 1939

PREPARATIONS

The Prime Minister had barely finished announcing the Declaration of War on the morning of 3rd September 1939, when the first air raid warning sounded in Wimbledon. All morning tearful parents, anxious to save their children from the holocaust that they thought would follow, had been packing them onto trains for evacuation to the country. The fear and dread that was felt when the sirens sounded can only be appreciated if one realises the strain under which everyone had lived for the previous few years.

The rise of Hitler since his appointment as Chancellor by President Hindenburg in 1933 had been watched with growing apprehension. In that year the German army expanded beyond the limit of 100,000 men set by the Versailles Treaty and re-armament began on a massive scale. The German Parliament Building, the Reichstag, was burnt down a month later and on the death of Hindenburg in August 1934 Hitler seized power as a dictator and the threat to the whole of Europe began to be realised. In 1935 Germany re-occupied the demilitarised zone of the Rhineland, repudiating the Locano Treaty, and in October of the same year the Italians demonstrated the effect of modern warfare against an unprepared nation when they attacked Abyssinia and the reports of poison gas attacks on unprotected civilians horrified the world. On 18th July 1936 civil war broke out in Spain and this provided Hitler with an opportunity to try out his newly formed dive-bomber squadrons against the civilian population of Guernica.

It was realised in Britain that if war came to this Country it would be necessary to have a trained organisation to deal with the personal suffering and total disruption that would follow the bombing of cities. The setting up of the ARP (Air Raid Precautions) service, later to be known as Civil Defence, was begun. In 1937 pamphlets were issued outlining the work to be carried out by the ARP and calling for volunteers. Plans were made for the evacuation of civilians and the construction of shelters and defence posts was put in hand.

In March 1938 a booklet had been issued entitled 'The Protection of your Home against Air Raids'. It gave advice on how to form a refuge-room within each house, sealed against gas and protected against blast and bomb splinters. Advice was also given on blacking out windows, precautions to be taken against fire and notes on basic first aid.

A number of Air Raid Wardens had now been trained and their first duty was to establish a personal relationship with the householders in their area and to explain to them the need for these precautions and preparations.

In March 1938 Austria was annexed by Germany and by September war seemed imminent. On 28th September the British Navy was mobilised but the following day a brief respite was obtained by the signing of the Munich Agreement. The Sudetenland (forming the outer fringe of Czechoslovakia's territories) was ceded to Germany on the grounds that the population was of German origin and on the assurance of Hitler that he would make no further territorial claims. But as most of Czechoslovakia's defence positions were in this area the rest of the country was left unprotected and a few months later Hitler marched his armies into Prague and claimed the remaining territories of Bohemia and Moravia as German Protectorates.

Preparations for the expected air raids in this country were now nearing completion. Underground shelters had been constructed in parks and open spaces and surface shelters of brick and concrete were built in side roads. The basements of large buildings and private cellars were strengthened and in the gardens of many houses corrugated steel Anderson shelters were being sunk into the ground and protected with earth and sandbags. At distribution centres, staffed by wardens and the WVS, there were queues for respirators, or gas masks as they were more generally known. For civilians there was a simple rubber face mask fitted with a filter, supplied with a cardboard carrying box. Later a supplementary filter was added to give protection against a wider range of gasses but since it contained asbestos fibre this probably did more harm than good.

ARP workers had already been issued with a respirator of stouter construction, which was carried in a canvas bag, and for firemen and rescue workers, who would be required to remain and work in danger areas for long periods, service respirators with canister filters were issued. There were red 'Mickey Mouse' respirators for small children and rubberised canvas breathing tents for babies. Examples of these can be seen in the Wimbledon Society's Local History Museum.

Following the conquest of Czechoslovakia, Hitler turned his attention to Poland. The Anglo-Polish Treaty was signed in May 1939 in the

Gas mask fitting

belief that protection by Great Britain would be enough to deter an attack on that country. But when Hitler invaded Poland on 1st September war between Great Britain and Germany became inevitable. The effect of Hitler's blitzkreig was shattering. Because the attack came without warning most of the Polish Air Force was destroyed before it could leave the ground. Without opposition in the air the Luftwaffe was able to reduce towns and cities to rubble within a few hours and the highly mechanised German army moved through the country with incredible speed. It was against this background that ARP wardens were now called upon to man their posts day and night in case an attack on this country should precede a formal declaration. Not all wardens' posts had been equipped or fitted with telephones and for many wardens it meant nights of sleeping on the floor and arranging a chain of verbal communications.

When the sirens sounded almost immediately after the declaration of war on 3rd September there was no panic but people took to their shelters or cellars fearing the worst. Ambulance and rescue teams stood by wearing full gas protective clothing and wardens toured the streets blowing their whistles as a warning to take cover. But this only caused

3

confusion because some people thought that the whistles signified a gas attack and put on their respirators. However, it was all over very quickly and the all clear sounded soon afterwards. It had been a false alarm caused by an unidentified aircraft but it was useful in that it showed up the weaknesses in the system.

In the days that followed cinemas, theatres and all other places that might attract large gatherings were closed. Schools were also closed for a while, partly for the same reason but also because many children had been evacuated. Some that had been depleted in this way amalgamated to provide temporary classes for children from several schools while they sorted out more permanent arrangements. Some independent schools moved to a new location in the country. With no further air raid warnings in the remaining months of 1939 life regained a semblance of normality but preparations continued.

The organisation of the ARP was the responsibility of the local authority and in 1939 an emergency committee had been formed. The Controller of the civil defence organisation, under whom came the heads of the various services, was the Town Clerk. At the beginning of the war this was Mr. Emmerson Smith but he was forced to retire due to ill health. Until his successor, Mr. Edwin Neave, was appointed the task of organising civil defence fell to the Deputy Town Clerk, Mr. Arthur Rolt. He was assisted by the Borough Surveyor, Mr. Tom Webster, who was also responsible for the Rescue Service and for communications throughout the war. The Chief Warden during the period of the air raids was Mr. George Ball who succeeded Sir Patrick Kelly in this post in 1940. The Council's full-time paid Civil Defence Officer, Captain Seymour, worked in close liaison with the Clerk to the Civil Defence Committee, Mr. F. Castleton. Mr. Neave was later awarded an OBE for his work as Controller.

The heart of the civil Defence Organisation was the Control Room, situated in the basement of the Town Hall at the Queens Road end of the building. In this Control Room were the Controller, the Borough Engineer, the Medical Officer of Health and representatives of the Fire Service and public utility undertakings. The Control Room had direct links by telephone to the Fire Station and Police Station nearby. Contact with the many wardens' posts, auxiliary fire stations, rescue centres, ambulance stations and first aid posts was maintained through the telephone room, which was positioned between the Control Room

4

and the Queens Road entrance. Under the front of the building were duty rooms, emergency stores and the rooms occupied by the Messenger Service who, with their own cars, motorbikes and bicycles, maintained communications when the telephone lines were out of action. They also used their cars to transport the survivors of bombing incidents to rest centres, hospitals or to mortuaries in order to identify those who had been killed.

A frequent visitor to the Control Room was Alderman A.W. Hickmott, who retired from the Council in 1960 after forty years unbroken service and who had been made a Freeman of the Borough in 1937. Whenever reports of damage or casualties came in he would go out on foot to offer aid and advice to those who had suffered in any part of the borough. His wife and Mrs. Webster set up a canteen in the Town Hall basement. This was greatly appreciated by all those who had to spend long hours on duty at the Control Centre.

Members of the Messenger Service outside the Town Hall

For Civil Defence purposes the Borough was divided into thirty-three ARP post areas. Later in the war the posts were organized into five districts with twenty-five post areas. As Chief Warden, Mr. Ball had eight hundred and seven wardens under his command, of whom one

5

hundred and thirty-three were employed full-time (at a weekly pay of £3) and six hundred and seventy-four were part-time volunteers. By the end of the war the total number had increased to one thousand and an additional six thousand firewatchers had been recruited. The air raid wardens formed the first line of defence and the direct link between the services and the civilian population. Men and women of all social backgrounds and walks of life worked closely together. They made friends with people in their post areas and came to be known and trusted. It was important for the wardens to know where people lived, where they sheltered and when they would be away from home. Searching the remains of a demolished building was dangerous work and knowing that a house was empty could save time and risk of injury. Wardens paid particular attention to people living on their own, to the old and to the infirm.

During air raids the wardens patrolled their areas and as soon as an incident occurred they would report details to their post, from which the information would be passed to the Control Centre at the Town Hall. Where fire was involved they could call directly to the Fire Brigade. The work of the various services at the incident was usually co-ordinated by the warden but when damage was widespread an Incident Officer would be sent from the Town Hall to take charge. The report, known as an M1, gave the location, details of the incident, an estimate of the number of casualties, the extent of the damage and the services required. Fire fighting equipment, ambulances and light and heavy rescue teams would then be sent as necessary. This process was later speeded up by the introduction of an Express Report, which preceded the M1 and gave only the location of the incident and the need for ambulance or fire service.

Wimbledon, however, had a system that was unique among all the London suburbs. From the roof of the Town Hall it was possible to see about seventy-five per cent of the borough. The Town Clerk and the Borough Engineer set up an observation post on the roof of the Town Hall with the points of the compass marked on a plotting table. From this post, bearings could be taken on most of the landmarks and road junctions throughout the borough. Mr. Webster originally arranged the manning of the post from his own department but later, when regular bombing started, the duty was taken over by a rota of forty specially trained wardens recruited from various parts of the borough. The

Ministry of Home Security rather frowned upon this scheme and objected to the expense incurred and the large number of wardens needed to man the post day and night. But when Mr. Webster was able to show what a tremendous help it was in locating incidents, the Ministry backed down.

Later, a second observation post was established on the roof of Eagle House in Wimbledon High Street. This not only gave a view of the remainder of the borough but also allowed cross bearings to be taken to give the location of any incident. Within a few seconds of a bomb falling its position could be pinpointed to within fifteen yards. One ambulance, usually driven by a woman, and a light rescue team would be sent immediately to the scene of the incident and these would often arrive before the air raid warden's report had reached the Control Centre.

The police and fire services retained their own organisations but appointed liaison officers to work with the civil defence organisation. One of the many duties of the police in connection with the raids was to keep track of those who had been killed, injured or were missing and they worked closely with the rescue service.

Mr. W.Y.Johnson, who was then the local building inspector, was responsible for the rescue service under Mr. Webster. At the beginning of the war their headquarters was set up at the Durnsford Road sewage works. There were eight light rescue teams, each of four men, and four heavy rescue teams of ten to twelve men. They were on duty in twenty-four hour shifts and at least one team attended every incident. The light rescue units were manned mainly by men from the ambulance service and they were provided with an ambulance or utility van with stretchers, picks, shovels and small lifting gear. There were many men from the building trade in the rescue service and they were mainly in the heavy rescue teams, which were equipped with heavy lifting gear and cutting equipment.

Mr. C.R.Gates, a local builder, was one of the supervisors and he gave instruction on working in damaged buildings and directed numerous rescue operations. Another supervisor was an explosives expert from the Royal Engineers with specialist knowledge of the demolition of buildings. In the autumn of 1940 the headquarters of the service was moved to Queens Road School, where it was housed in an annex, and a gas contamination building was constructed in the school

7

grounds. The light rescue section was reorganised and expanded into four teams comprising ten men in each. From this centre the service operated without interruption, in spite of the destruction of many ambulances and rescue vehicles by high explosive bombs in November and by incendiary bombs in December 1940. At the end of the blitz in 1941 the rescue service was moved to the Council Depot in Queens Road.

The work carried out by the rescue teams was both hard and harrowing and often left the men physically and mentally exhausted. It involved not only the rescue of survivors but also the removal of bodies and parts of mutilated bodies from the wreckage. Although over a period of time many of them became hardened to this work they could not always control their emotions, especially when the bodies of small children were uncovered in the debris. The supervisor of the rescue team had to keep a close watch on his men who were often working to the limit of their endurance. Mr. Gates recalled that one of his men would regularly faint when called out to an incident. The other members of his team would simply put him on a stretcher and load him into the ambulance and by the time they arrived at the incident he would have regained consciousness. It was this same man who was always the first to volunteer to crawl into an unsupported tunnel to pull out anyone who was trapped.

Members of the Fire Brigade worked closely with the Rescue Service and were often able to help in locating people who were injured and trapped under the rubble. During the heavy raids on Lambeth and Lewisham, fire fighting and rescue teams from Wimbledon were sent to help the local services in those areas. Later in the war, when rescue teams in Wimbledon were working day and night, reinforcements were brought from Mitcham and from as far away as Salisbury, Newark and Market Harborough.

Part-time auxiliary firemen augmented the regular fire brigade and the main appliances were supplemented by utility vans with trailer pumps. In this way the service was increased to ten times its normal peacetime strength. The trailer pumps were efficient, compact units, powered by Coventry Climax engines (the same engines that were later to be the foundation of British motor racing success after the war).

Auxiliary fire unit with trailer pump at Wimbledon Fire Station.

But even with the backing of auxiliary firemen and appliances, a local fire service could not hope to deal with all the fires that might occur simultaneously in a heavy raid and so the fire service in Greater London was organised on a very wide flexible basis. Appliances were called out through a central operations room where a careful check was kept on the situation. As the pattern of the raid became clear and before the local fire brigade was stretched to its limit, reserves of men and appliances would be called in from neighbouring districts and they in turn would be replaced by units from further afield. During the heavy raids on London, reserves converged on the City from as far away as Bristol, Birmingham and Northampton.

A documentary film, 'Fires were started', which illustrated life in an auxiliary fire station during the blitz, was later entered into a European film festival. It was rejected as being unrealistic because it showed the firemen singing and cracking jokes around a piano before going out to face possible death. The spirit of the time was summed up by the comedian Rob Wilton who, playing the part of an auxiliary fireman said, "We really should get a telephone. I'm sure there are lots of fires we never even hear about."

Fire stations and ambulance stations were set up at local schools, halls and even houses. Mobile first aid units were formed which were often taken to major incidents to provide immediate treatment for the injured. These mobile units were equipped for emergency operations but serious cases were usually sent to the local first aid post or directly to hospital. Dr. Harold Ellis, Medical Officer of Health for Wimbledon, headed the first aid section and he was assisted by Dr. Patrick Doody, later to be MOH for the London Borough of Merton. When Dr. Doody was called into the armed services in November 1940, his duties were taken over by Dr. C.S.Cloake. Most local doctors had assignments at hospitals or first aid posts during air raids. Others were free to emulate the practice of Dr. Doody who attended serious incidents and administered pain killing drugs or heart stimulants to trapped casualties. This often involved crawling under the debris of demolished buildings, with the added difficulty that much of the work had to be carried out in absolute darkness. When an incident doctor was not available the responsibility for diagnosing the severity of injuries and the immediate treatment to be given fell to the first aid workers who had Red Cross, St. John's or St. Andrew's training.

The main ambulance stations were at Cottenham Park Church Hall, under the direction of Miss Margaret Roney, and at Queens Road School, with Dr. Cloake in attendance. At first there were very few ambulances so all types of vehicle were pressed into service. At the Cottenham Park ambulance station there were several private cars, two furniture vans and two vehicles that had been used for transporting greyhounds to Wimbledon Stadium. The private cars were used by stretcher parties and for transporting casualties with minor injuries and

10

additional ambulances were constructed by building square van bodies onto car chassis. At the beginning of the war there were a number of men in the ambulance service but most of these were called up and the service became staffed almost entirely by women. Duty was originally organised in twelve-hour shifts but later the shifts became twenty-four hours in duration.

First aid stations were established at Pelham Road School, under Sister Rosie and at the pavilion on the Oberon Playing Fields, Lindisfarne Road, under Sister Wadey. At the All England Tennis Club, where treating the injured had taken the place of tennis tournaments, Club Sister Rutter was in charge.

Staff and visitors at the 'All England' first aid post. On the left, Dr.C.S. Cloak, Mr. Alfred Munns (Civil Defence Officer), Alderman Drake (The Mayor) and behind him Mr. Edwin Neave (Town Clerk and ARP Controller), centre, Admiral Evans of the Broke (ARP Commissioner for S.E. England), behind him Dr. Harold Ellis (MOH), Miss Rutter (Nursing Sister in charge) and at the rear right, Mr. George Ball (Chief Warden).

The Centre Court also served as a mortuary but fewer people were killed in the bombing than had been expected so the stacks of cardboard coffins that had been hastily manufactured remained largely unused.

Finding accommodation for those who survived became the major problem. Public halls were used as temporary rest centres. Wimbledon Village Hall in Lingfield Road was divided into cubicles to house many homeless families. The rest centres were organised and managed by the WVS who looked after and fed people until they could be found accommodation by the Billeting Officer. On major incidents they worked with the wardens to set up enquiry points or Blitz Information Bureaux. In the nearest habitable building to the incident an office would be established and equipment moved in, including a first aid kit and supplies of hot chocolate. From these points help and advice could be given to the stunned survivors and information to the relatives of those who were casualties. The WVS also took upon themselves the duty of finding homes for pets, because no animals were allowed in the rest centres.

Rations, clothing and furniture had to be provided for those who had lost all their possessions and a large clothing depot was set up in Raymond Road where the WVS cleaned, sorted and repaired second-hand clothing for distribution to victims of the bombing. Later in the war gifts of clothing and toys came from America and Canada and gifts of furniture came from the City of Leicester, which adopted Wimbledon during the flying bomb period and to which many Wimbledon children were evacuated. During 1940, when large numbers of refugees from Poland, Belgium, Holland and France arrived in Wimbledon, the WVS was ready and waiting to receive and feed them at Wimbledon Stadium, where they were billeted until accommodation could be found.

Mrs. Margaret Sargent, who was Deputy to Dr. Grace Winn, organised a housewives service throughout the borough. In almost every street, groups of housewives were formed who, with basic training in first aid, could assist at incidents in their area.

It would be difficult to list all the duties performed by the WVS but above all they provided those simple human things that were not covered by official planning.

Miss Margaret Roney (right) with members of the Cottenham Park ambulance station and one of their first ambulances adapted from a newsagent's delivery van.

THE STAGE IS SET

The air raid sirens had sounded for the first time immediately after the declaration of war but after this false alarm very little happened until the late spring of 1940. This period, lasting eight months, became known as the phoney war. As there appeared to be no sign of the threatened air attacks, theatres and cinemas opened again, schools returned to normal and many evacuees came home. Exercises were organised to train air raid wardens and members of the greatly expanded fire and ambulance services but these were regarded as necessary precautions rather than as a response to any serious threat.

It was not until Hitler invaded France in May 1940 that the people of Britain were awakened to the real threat that faced them. On 14th May 1940, the Local Defence Volunteer Force (later to be known as the Home Guard) was set up. They had no uniforms and no firearms, apart from a few shotguns, and volunteers came mainly from those who were too young or too old to be called up into the regular armed forces. Recruits were given armbands to wear over their civilian suits and carried out rifle drill using broomsticks for rifles. It is hardly surprising, therefore, that at first they were not taken very seriously. The comedian Rob Wilton recalled telling his wife that he had joined the Home Guard and that if the Germans invaded it would be his job to stop them. "What, you?" she asked, incredulously. "Oh no," he assured her. "Not just me. There are seven or eight of us."

The 54th Surrey Battalion of the Home Guard was formed under Lieut. Colonel W.P.C. Tenison and comprised men from Wimbledon, Merton and Morden. Its headquarters was at the Old Drill Hall in St. George's Road, backing onto the railway, and it was here that they had their officers' mess, storeroom and rifle range. They also used the rifle range at Rutlish School in the Kingston Road. There were eight companies in the Battalion and it fell to the lot of C Company, under the command of Major Stapleton Harris, to guard Wimbledon Common. The Company Headquarters was at No.3 Parkside Gardens. The common was used for training and there were regular all-night patrols, especially during the period of the Blitz. The Home Guard also helped the police and civil defence services, standing guard over unexploded bombs and bomb-damaged buildings.

14

The 54th Surrey Battalion of the Home Guard on Wimbledon Common.

On 13th June the ringing of church bells was banned except as a warning of invasion. A pillbox was built within the old pound at the junction of Parkside and Cannizaro Road and some roads were restricted in width by pyramid shaped concrete blocks known as dragon's teeth to obstruct tanks. Trenches were dug across parts of the Common, both as defensive positions and to prevent aircraft landing. The Home Guard also made use of an assault course built by the regular army near Rushmere. Uniforms and firearms had now been issued but the ability of the Home Guard to make a stand against a well trained and better-equipped invading army has to be doubted.

It was recognised at higher levels that rather than using the Home Guard as cannon fodder in direct combat against superior forces they could be used as guerrilla fighters, attacking by stealth. Unarmed combat training was introduced and a special school was set up at Osterley Park where fighters who had gained experience of such tactics in the Spanish Civil War could train Home Guard units. They taught the Home Guard how to be self sufficient, manufacturing their own explosives and incendiary devices and how to strangle unsuspecting guards with piano wire. However, the powers that be had second thoughts about this when they realised that all these Civil War veterans were rampant Communists and the unit was closed down. Instead of general training for guerrilla warfare, small groups were selected to go into hiding in secret underground shelters from which they could launch rearguard attacks against a successful invading force. These were suicide squads and the secrecy that surrounded them has seldom been broken. It is not known if there were any in this area but the Common would have provided ideal opportunities for such shelters. What is known is that the German invasion plans included the removal of most of the trees from Wimbledon Common and its development as the main airfield for London. Houses along Parkside were to have been commandeered for use by Luftwaffe crews and staff.

The campaign in France was over very quickly. Unlike the First World War, when troops dug themselves into the ground and faced each other across a strip of open land for months on end, it was a war of rapid movement. The German Luftwaffe made the first move, attacking their opponents' airfields and destroying aircraft before they could get into the air. This was followed with motorised troops and tanks over-running or skirting around the fixed defensive positions and once this momentum had built up it was difficult to stop. Thus almost before we realised what was happening most of the RAF aircraft stationed in France had been destroyed and our expeditionary force was being driven back to the sea.

Because of the losses and the need to retain sufficient fighters to defend Britain, Air Chief Marshall Sir Hugh Dowding, Chief of Fighter Command (who lived at 3 St. Mary's Road, Wimbledon) had argued against sending more and more reinforcements to France but Churchill overruled him and by the time France surrendered on 22nd June 1940 we had lost 959 aircraft, 509 of these being fighters. Also 435 pilots had been killed, injured or taken prisoner and these would be more difficult to replace than the aircraft. At this point there were only 331 Spitfires and Hurricanes left to defend Britain with some second line fighters such as Blenheims, Defiants and Gladiator biplanes.

Following the evacuation from Dunkirk at the end of May 1940, Hitler had assumed that the war was over and disbanded fifteen divisions of the German army. He could not believe that after such a defeat Britain could refuse his generous terms for peace. He relaxed, toured his conquered territories and consolidated his gains. It was not until July, when it became clear that Britain did not consider itself defeated and intended to continue the war against Germany, that he considered invading England. The Battle of Britain was the first stage of this operation.

Previously all his campaigns had been fought on land and, although the English Channel was only twenty miles wide, an invasion by sea presented new problems. Hitler consulted his chiefs of staff and it was Admiral Raeder who came up with the best solution.

Germany had no landing craft and had to improvise using Rhine barges. These needed to be assembled at the Channel ports and then towed across the Channel at a speed of about 3 knots. They would be vulnerable to attack from both sea and air and therefore had to be protected. The main invasion would take place between Brighton and Dover and head north to London with a secondary force landing at Portland. Paratroops were to be dropped just behind the beaches to secure the area ready for the barges to unload their troops, tanks and supplies. The slow barges would be protected by E-boats and by minefields laid on each side to prevent attacks from warships. U-boats were to be deployed as an outer defence to prevent larger warships using their long-range guns. British warships would also have to be kept busy defending themselves against attacks from German aircraft but this could only happen if the RAF had been put out of action.

Eliminating opposition from the air was part of the normal tactics of blitzkrieg used by Germany against every country it had invaded. Herman Goering, Commander in Chief of the Luftwaffe, was convinced that it would take only a week or two to eliminate the RAF.

The Battle of Britain is still remembered by the British as a separate event whereas the Germans saw it as part of their overall invasion plan. In fact it was not known as the Battle of Britain at the time; the name first appeared as the title of a leaflet published by the Air Ministry in 1941. The phrase came from a speech made by Churchill after the fall of France in which he said, "The Battle of France is over, the Battle of Britain is about to begin." At that time he was not referring to an air battle.

While preparations were made for the invasion, the Luftwaffe began to attack shipping in the English Channel. The campaign, known to the Germans as Kanalkampf, had started on 1st July 1940 and was to last until 8th August. Convoys of coastal shipping were particularly vulnerable. On 25th July a convoy set sail from the Thames estuary and

17

out of 21 ships only two survived. Similarly on 8th August another convoy set out from Southend at night heading for Swanage and out of 24 ships only four arrived at their destination. These terrible losses were pointless and unnecessary. The ships were carrying coal, which could easily have been sent by rail. The Government was just trying to prove that we still had control over the English Channel, which we clearly did not. The public heard nothing of these losses but did have running commentaries on the radio describing the aerial combat. The score for each side was given with the excitement usually reserved for reporting goals in a football match.

Apart from damage to shipping the aim of the Kanalkampf attacks was to draw the RAF units into the air so that they could be shot down over the sea. During the Battle of France, RAF aircrew were at a disadvantage because if they baled out they were likely to land in enemy occupied territory and be taken prisoner. Now if they baled out they were likely to drown. In fact drowning became the most common cause of death for RAF pilots during this period. If a pilot did manage to escape from his damaged aircraft he then had to use his parachute and hope he was at a sufficient height for it to open. He would have had no previous experience of using a parachute because training carried too great a risk of injury and there was a shortage of pilots. On the way down he had to blow into a tube on his life-jacket to inflate it and remember to loosen his tie and undo the collar of his shirt because in the water the tie would expand and choke him. Kicking off flying boots was also advisable because once filled with water they were like anchors. Finally just before he hit the water the pilot would have to jettison his parachute. If he failed to do so it would collapse on top of him, become waterlogged and drag him down. Life expectancy in the cold water was just four hours. If pilots were injured or unconscious their chances of survival were small and if they did manage to stay afloat the chance of being picked up by one of the six air-sea rescue launches that had to cover the whole of the English coastline was remote.

When German pilots were shot down they had a much better chance of survival. They had a self-inflating life-jacket and a one-man inflatable dinghy; they wore a bright yellow skull-cap under their flying helmet and had a packet of yellow dye that would spread in the water around them. Also there were German rescue buoys floating in the

Channel and if they could reach one of these or their yellow marker dye was spotted from the air they would be picked up by a regular service of Dornier flying boats. Although these flying boats carried Red Cross markings our pilots were ordered to shoot them down on the basis that they would be carrying 'aircrew on active service'.

Within three weeks 220 RAF pilots had died including 80 experienced Flight and Squadron Commanders; and this was before the 'Battle of Britain' had begun.

On 16th July 1940 Hitler issued his Directive 16 in which he stated, *"Since England, in spite of her hopeless military situation, shows no sign of being ready to come to a compromise, I have decided to prepare a landing operation against England and, if necessary, to carry it out."* The operation was given the designation Seelöwe (Sea Lion) and was planned for the latter part of August or September. There were only two periods when the tides and moon would be right for an invasion, 20th to 26th August and 19th to 26th September, and preparations for those dates were put in hand.

Adlertag (Eagle Day), the launch of the air attacks leading up to the invasion, was fixed for 13th August 1940. This gave Herman Goering seven to twelve days in which to destroy the RAF before the first suitable invasion date and more than a month before the September deadline.

Heavy guns near the Windmill on Wimbledon Common.

19

THE FIRST AIR RAIDS

On 11th and 12th August 1940, in preparation for Eagle Day, the German Luftwaffe attempted to knock out the radar stations that they knew were important to our defences. However, these targets proved to be very difficult for them because the stations themselves were quite small buildings and the radar masts, which were lattice structures like giant electricity pylons, allowed the blast from bombs to pass through them without doing much damage.

Tuesday 13th August 1940 started with heavy rain and poor visibility so the German attack was officially called off. When the weather began to clear a number of German squadrons took off but the attack was disorganised due to poor radio communications. Some bomber pilots found they had no fighter escort while fighter pilots found themselves with no bombers to protect. By mistake their radios had been set to different frequencies.

There was little activity on the 14th when the weather was again bad but on 15th August 520 German bombers crossed the coast to continue their attacks on airfields and radar installations in south-east England. The blue summer sky was criss-crossed with white vapour trails and for the first time Croydon became a target. In fact it was probably not the intended target because it appears to have been mistaken for the Fighter Command station at Kenley, a few miles south.

Before the war Croydon was an international airport for civilian aircraft and it had only recently been taken over by the RAF. Soon after their arrival an officer in the control tower had picked up a telephone and replaced it hastily when he was answered in German. It was still connected on a direct line to Templehof aerodrome.

Officers were housed in the Aerodrome Hotel and other ranks in the Imperial Airways hanger while part of the Terminal building was used to store ammunition. Another way in which Croydon differed from other RAF stations was that it was in a town rather than open country and had many houses and industrial buildings around it.

During the raid that started at 7.30 that evening three hangers were hit and the armoury in the Terminal building was destroyed, killing six airmen. But it was the civilian population that suffered most when houses and buildings on the adjoining industrial estate were hit. Altogether sixty-two people were killed and one hundred and seventy-four injured. The air raid had lasted only thirty minutes but the pall of smoke left hanging over Croydon could be seen clearly from Wimbledon.

The next day, Friday 16th August, it was Wimbledon's turn to experience the battle at close quarters. There was an alert just after mid-day that lasted for fifty minutes and at 5.15 pm the sirens sounded again. After a year of 'phoney war' life had almost returned to normal and the theatre and cinemas were open again. At the Elite (ABC) Cinema in Wimbledon Broadway the film 'Just William' was playing to a large audience of children. It may seem strange, after the devastation caused at Croydon on the previous day, that few people seem to have been concerned about the possible dangers but then most of them did not know what had really happened. The BBC had falsely reported that in the Croydon raid only one person had been killed and that all the German aircraft taking part had been shot down!

At the cinema an announcement was made from the stage that a warning had been sounded and some of those present left the building to take shelter. Ten minutes later the first bombs fell a few hundred yards away and within minutes fourteen people had been killed and fifty-nine injured. The bombs were small, only 50 kg., and they fell roughly along the line of Merton High Street and Kingston Road. Houses in Cecil Road and Montague Road were wrecked and in Palmerston Road all houses from No.72 to 106 and from 101 to 115 were damaged. In Russell Road No. 86, 131 and 143 were hit by bombs and all houses from 47 to 113 were damaged by blast. A car standing in the road burst into flames. Two 9 year old girls, Rosina and Audrey, were on their way home from Dundonald School when the warning sounded. One lived in Pelham Road and the other in Gladstone Road. As they passed through the slips at Bertram Cottages someone opened a door and offered them shelter but as they were so close to home they declined the offer. At the corner of Pelham and Gladstone Roads they parted and Audrey went to her home at 104 Gladstone Road. There was no one at home but at that moment she saw her mother with her younger brother and sister returning from shopping in the Broadway. They entered the house together just as the bomb fell. The two younger children survived, their mother lost her left arm and Audrey died from her wounds later that night.

21

Other bombs falling in Gladstone Road caused damage to No.74 and from 84 to 116 as well as houses on the other side of the road. The Wimbledon Tyre Company premises, at the corner of Montague Road and Kingston Road, received a direct hit and a fire was started in which several people died. The burning rubber produced heavy clouds of black smoke and another fire was started at the nearby Berne Motor Company in Kingston Road. In Hartfield Road there was a direct hit on No.135, a doctor's surgery, and all houses from 131 to 157 and from 158 to 168 were badly damaged. St. Andrew's Church in Herbert Road was spattered with machine gun bullets and bomb splinters hit several houses. In Graham Road, No.120 and 122 were partly demolished and adjoining houses on both sides of the road were badly damaged. When the warning sounded 14 year old Terence Rosewell, who lived at 101 Graham Road, was returning from having escorted an elderly family friend to her home. As he ran the last hundred yards three bombs fell, one ahead of him, one behind him and one on the pavement opposite. As he lay unconscious from his injuries the family, who were devout Catholics, sent for a priest who arrived using the bicycle of a neighbour who had been sent to meet him. Although he regained consciousness for a time the boy died from his wounds later that night.

Another bomb fell on the railway line, just north of the level crossing, at the rear of houses in Kingswood Road and electricity cables, gas and water mains were broken. Craters or debris blocked some roads but the Kingston Road was only rendered impassable for a short time, although bombs falling in the adjoining Merton area had damaged many buildings. Before the smoke had cleared the Civil Defence services had arrived and with them came the sightseers. This was the first air raid that most people had experienced and there was more curiosity than fear among those who had not been directly affected. The raid showed up several weaknesses in the Civil Defence system. Finding and listing the names of injured persons proved to be the greatest difficulty. Many were taken to hospitals and first aid posts without any record having been given to the wardens' post and at one incident, because there was no ambulance available, a badly injured woman was sent to hospital on the back of a coal cart. Other problems that had not been anticipated were the crowds of sightseers, who hampered rescue work, and the looters who searched the wreckage for valuables.

The spirit of 1940

An appeal was launched for aluminium saucepans to be melted down to make fighters. In Wimbledon the WVS collected more than six tons.

However, morale was high. After the raid hundreds of flags appeared at windows of houses in neighbouring streets. An antiques shop in Kingston Road that had been at the heart of the bombing put out a sign saying, "We buy anything second-hand, except broken glass." A nearby off-licence had the slogan "Fags and Beer – we are all here." Shortly after the raid a warden visited a house in Hardy Road where a delayed action bomb was thought to have fallen. On arrival he found a woman digging in her front garden who told him that she wanted whatever had fallen there as a souvenir!

In Kingston Road, wardens from the Merton area called in their opposite numbers from the Wimbledon post for consultation on a strange kink that had appeared in the railway line, close to the signal box by the level crossing. One of the wardens mentioned that the ballast appeared to have been disturbed and a railway worker, who was standing nearby, said, "When I came along after the raid there was a damn great hole there, so I filled it in and made it tidy." Fortunately the

24

bomb had a very long delay fuse and there was time to evacuate people from the houses nearby.

The story was also told of an old man who was found wandering among the ruins holding a lavatory chain. "All I did was pull it," he said, "and the whole bloody house fell down."

Semi-detached living in South Wimbledon after the raid of 5th April 1940.

THE AIRCRAFT

OUR DEFENCE

Although Wimbledon prepared for the invasion with its local Home Guard, tank traps, pillboxes and machine-gun posts, the attacks it had to face came from the air. The fact that Britain survived these attacks was largely due to private initiatives. The well-known Spitfires and Hurricanes and the Merlin engines that powered them were not built to Air Ministry specifications; they were all the result of work by far-sighted individuals.

In the 1920s and 30s the RAF was equipped with biplanes constructed mainly of wood and fabric. Their strength came from the fact that their two wings were strutted and braced with cables like a large box kite. Because the wings were short the aircraft were very manoeuvrable and having two wings gave them plenty of lift but also produced more drag, slowing them down. The fixed undercarriage did not help either. The Hawker Hart, introduced in 1930 as a light bomber, had a top speed of 184 mph and the fighter version that followed was only 3 mph faster.

The Gloucester Gladiator, built to Air Ministry specifications, was also a biplane with fixed undercarriage, radial engine, four machine-guns and a top speed of 257 mph. It was delivered to the RAF as their new front line fighter in 1937, two years before the war began. Fortunately, Reginald Mitchell of Vickers-Supermarine and Sydney Camm, chief designer for Hawker, had other ideas.

Mitchell had designed the Supermarine S6, the aircraft that broke the world air speed record at 407 mph in 1931 and made Britain outright winner of the Schneider Trophy. He was therefore well placed to design the world's best fighter aircraft. The Spitfire was an all-metal, low wing monoplane in which the metal skin of the airframe gave it its strength. The shape of the aircraft was dictated by the need for speed and manoeuvrability. The wingspan could be kept down to 11m (36ft) because the broad curved shape gave sufficient lift. The wheels retracted outward into the wings. The problem of obtaining a strong joint between the wing and the fuselage was resolved by using a main wing spar that ran through the body and was built up like a leaf spring. As with his trophy winning aircraft, Mitchell used a Rolls Royce

26

engine. The Merlin engine, developed by Sir Henry Royce, was again the result of a personal initiative rather than an Air Ministry specification. In fact its original designation was PV1, the PV standing for 'private venture'. This 1,030 h.p. engine gave the Spitfire a top speed of 362 mph.

At the same time that the Spitfire was being developed, Sydney Camm was already producing the Hawker Hurricane. This was not such an innovative design and was based upon Hawker biplanes with their traditional wood and fabric construction. However, without the strength provided by the struts and bracing of a biplane there was again the problem of obtaining a strong joint between the wing and the fuselage. Camm solved this by giving the Hurricane a tubular metal chassis inside the fuselage and extending it for a short distance into the wing on each side. This metal cage provided a strong fixing for the undercarriage, which folded inwards under the body, and space for fuel tanks in the wing roots. At 12.2m (40ft) the wings were longer and thicker than the Spitfire's so that although the Hurricane used the same Rolls Royce engine it had a top speed of only 328 mph. During the Battle the Hurricane was responsible for bringing down 80% of the German aircraft destroyed. This is partly because the number of Hurricanes far exceeded the number of Spitfires but also because Hurricanes were normally targeted against bombers while Spitfires were directed against their fighter escorts.

The other aircraft involved in the early stage of the battle was the Boulton-Paul Defiant. This looked rather like a Hurricane but with a revolving gun turret behind the pilot. This hydraulic turret allowed the guns to be swivelled to fire to the side or rear and this took some German pilots by surprise. However, the turret added a tonne to the weight of the aircraft, which made it slower and less manoeuvrable than other fighters. It soon had to be withdrawn due to heavy losses.

THE OPPOSITION

The German Messerschmitt Bf 109 E was another private venture. Willy Messerschmitt developed it from a small touring aircraft that he had designed. Like the Spitfire, it was a low wing monoplane of all metal construction but it was smaller and simpler to build than either the Spitfire or the Hurricane.

The Supermarine Spitfire was the fastest and most robust fighter of its time.

The German Messerschmitt Bf 109 E was smaller and lighter than the Spitfire and Hurricane and had a slightly more powerful engine.

Three Me 109's could be built in the time it took to build one Spitfire. If the Spitfire was the Rolls Royce of fighters then the Messerschmitt 109 was the Henry Ford of fighters. It had a wing-span of only 9.75m (32ft) compared to the Spitfire's 11m (36 ft) and the Hurricane's 12.2m (40ft) and weighed 30% less. It needed to be small and light because when it was first produced the only engine available was the Jumo engine producing 670 h.p. However, in 1938 a new Daimler-Benz 12 cylinder engine became available and this produced 1,150 h.p. (120 h.p. more than the Merlin). At first it appeared impossible to fit this large engine into such a small airframe but it was achieved by turning the engine upside down. This was possible because it was a fuel injection engine and the fuel supply did not rely upon gravity. However, with the heavier engine it was difficult to get sufficient lift from the Messerschmitt's small wings for take off, so these were fitted with automatic leading-edge slots. This was a Handley Page invention that directed the air more efficiently over the wing at low speeds but although it had been designed in Britain it was not used on British aircraft at that time. The power to weight ratio of the Me 109E enabled it to climb faster than a Spitfire and to operate at a height of 36,000 ft., nearly a mile higher.

It was at this time that Squadron Leader Sorley, at the Air Ministry, realised that with aircraft converging at a combined speed of 500-600 mph they would have only a split second in which to fire at each other. They would therefore have to have a massive amount of firepower and he recommended that the new fighters should each be fitted with eight machine-guns. For the Hurricane this was no problem; the wings were thick enough and long enough to accommodate the machine-guns and their ammunition. For the Spitfire it was more difficult because the wings were slimmer and the undercarriage retracted outwards into the wings. However, eight machine-guns were fitted, although they had to be well spaced out along each wing. The guns of both aircraft had to be angled inward so that the streams of bullets would converge at a point 200 yards ahead. To achieve maximum firepower, therefore, the pilot not only had to aim at his target but also to be the right distance from it. Too close and the streams of bullets would not have converged; too far and they would be spreading out again. Some pilots had their guns realigned to meet at 100 yards.

The news that British fighters were being fitted with eight machine-guns came as a shock to the Germans. The Me 109 was fitted with only two, mounted above the engine, with the possibility of fitting a 20mm canon to fire through the propeller boss (this was later dropped because it interfered with the running of the engine). The wings were short and very slim so it was not possible to fit a row of machine-guns into them. Fitting one 20mm canon into each wing, with a bulge underneath to take the ammunition box solved the problem. Again, by innovation, the Germans had managed to turn a problem into an advantage. One cannon shell weighed 14 times as much as a machine-gun bullet, so in spite of having fewer guns the hitting power of the Me 109 became nearly double that of a Spitfire or Hurricane. The Hurricanes and Spitfires carried enough ammunition to fire for only 15 seconds. The Me 109's canons could fire for just 7 seconds but its two machine-guns could continue for nearly a minute.

The one weakness of the Me 109 was its very light construction. This led some German pilots to avoid the extreme aerobatics of which it was capable for fear of breaking off the wings or the tail plane. On at least one occasion a British fighter pilot, having run out of ammunition, used his wing tip to break off the tail of a Me 109.

Another fighter used in the battle was the Messerschmitt Bf 110. This was a much larger, twin-engine aircraft with a wingspan of 16m (53ft). With four machine-guns and two cannons mounted in the nose it had formidable firepower but it was not as manoeuvrable as either the Spitfire or the Hurricane. This aircraft was also used as a dive-bomber and later, when fitted with radar, as a night fighter.

The German bombers used in the attacks on Britain were of four main types. All were of medium size and designed for the role of softening up targets prior to invasion rather than obliterating them. If these had been long-range heavy bombers, of the type that were later developed by Britain to attack targets deep in enemy territory, the damage they caused could have been much greater.

The principal bombers used against us were the Dornier 17, the Heinkel 111 and the Junkers 87 and 88. All, except the Ju 87, were twin engine, mid-wing aircraft. The Dornier Do.17Z, sometimes known as the flying pencil because of its slim body, was originally designed to carry airmail. It had a wingspan of 18m (59ft) and carried a bomb load of only 1,000 kg. It had a top speed of 265 mph so our fighters were nearly 100 mph faster.

The Heinkel 111 was the largest of these bombers, with a wingspan of 22.6m (74ft) and carried a bomb load of 2,000 kg. Like the Dornier it was comparatively slow, having a top speed of 258 mph, and in spite of its heavy armour plating it was vulnerable to fighters.

The best of the German bombers was the Junkers Ju 88. Its wingspan of 18m (59ft) was similar to the Dornier but it was of much more advanced design and has sometimes been compared to the British Mosquito bomber. Unlike the other bombers it carried its bomb load of 1,800 kg. externally, under the wings. Its top speed of 286 mph was produced by two 1,200 h.p. Jumo engines but these were later replaced by BMW engines.

Finally, the Junkers Ju 87 or Stuka was a single engine low-wing monoplane with a fixed undercarriage. It was designed specifically for the role of dive-bombing. It carried a 500 kg. bomb under the fuselage on a framework that was lowered before release so that it would clear the propeller during a steep dive. Also there were four 50 kg. bombs carried under the wings. This was a cumbersome looking aircraft but was designed for very accurate bombing and as a psychological weapon. On arriving at his target the pilot would put the aircraft into a near vertical dive and aim his 500 kg bomb through a glazed panel in the floor of the aircraft. It was used mainly against shipping and to pinpoint targets such as road junctions and railway lines. To achieve such accuracy it had to have very large air brakes on the wings to slow it down. However, to make it seem more formidable it was fitted with sirens that produced a rising scream as it dived and the bombs themselves were fitted with whistles on the tail fins. The slowness of its attack (about 100 mph) made it very vulnerable to our fighters and it had to be withdrawn from service after massive losses during its unsuccessful attacks on radar stations.

Although none of these aircraft was able to carry a very heavy bomb load, their bases in Belgium and France were so close to London that they were able to re-fuel and re-load and make two or three raids in one day or night.

THE TACTICS

The German bombers flew in tight formation, on the basis that there was safety in numbers. Although each of the bombers was lightly armed they could bring their combined firepower to bear on any attackers. The German fighters accompanying them flew at a higher altitude so that they could dive onto any attacking force. At first our fighters flew in tight formations, as they had always done in peace time air displays, but it made them easier to see from a distance, unlike the German fighters, which flew in a much looser formation of two pairs. Also flying closely together meant that British pilots had to keep a close eye on each other to avoid collisions, so they had less time to search for the enemy. The best way for a fighter to attack a bomber was to dive onto it from behind, pull out of the dive underneath it and fire up into its underside. However, there was always the chance that a German fighter would be on your tail doing exactly the same to you. Some squadrons developed a new and dangerous tactic of flying head on into the bomber formation causing it to break up or face a head-on collision.

When diving to get away from a German fighter, Hurricanes and Spitfires were at a disadvantage because the high negative G force produced by this manoeuvre caused their Merlin engines to misfire. The Messerschmitt, with its fuel injection engine, did not have this problem. To overcome their handicap the British fighters would perform a half roll so that they could dive inverted but this manoeuvre gave away their intention to the pursuing aircraft. Some pilots developed a crafty technique in which they did a quarter roll but then climbed instead of diving. On seeing the roll the German pilot would start to dive in anticipation but then find that the Spitfire or Hurricane was above instead of below him.

In spite of these tactics, in fighter-to-fighter combat the British losses were almost always greater that the German. It was only the RAF's success in shooting down German bombers that redressed the balance. As the battle progressed, the bomber pilots complained that they were not receiving sufficient protection from their fighters so Herman Goering ordered his fighter squadrons to provide closer support. This was a serious mistake because it meant that the fighters had to fly alongside the bombers at a slower speed and lower height giving our fighters a big advantage.

THE BATTLE

There were no air raids on the day following the first attack on Wimbledon but the sirens sounded again early in the afternoon of Sunday 18th August 1940. There was some anti-aircraft fire and sounds of bombing from the direction of Croydon. In fact the main attacks of that day were concentrated on the airfields at Kenley and Biggin Hill. On the 19th the weather changed and for four days a heavy layer of cloud protected the south of England. Three alerts sounded during the night of 24th August, the first night of bombing on London, and from then on the air raids became more frequent by day and night. The intensity of the attacks is reflected in the fact that during the twelve days from 26th August to 6th September, 322 German aircraft were brought down for the loss of 248 RAF fighters.

However, no further bombs fell in Wimbledon until the night of Sunday 8th September. In the Civil Defence incident reports this is recorded as raid No.2 but in the fifteen days from 24th August to 8th September the air raid sirens had sounded 46 times, each alert lasting from half an hour to as much as seven hours. Throughout the evening of the 7th there was the continuous sound of aircraft, anti-aircraft guns and machine-gun fire. The raid lasted until the following morning and the sky was lit by many searchlights and by the glow of a great fire that spread across the sky from the direction of East London, where the docklands were being attacked. The following night the fires in London were still burning and detachments of firemen and rescue workers from Wimbledon had been sent to assist. A few minutes after 11.0 pm bombs again fell in the Wimbledon area.

The bombs fell mainly around the station, the first landing on the District Railway track beside platform 1. An approaching train managed to stop in time but there were nine casualties, including the driver. The marks of the bomb splinters can still be seen in the concrete wall facing the platform. At the other side of the railway bridge a cottage, No.10 Railway Place, received a direct hit and other bombs exploded in gardens at the rear of No.54 Alexandra Road and No.18 Woodside. Thirty-five people who were rendered homeless found shelter in the William Morris Hall at the far end of the Broadway and were provided with breakfast at the YMCA opposite. Oil bombs were reported to have fallen on the railway bank near Strathearn Road and on

33

the footpath of Durnsford Road Bridge. These were large but primitive forms of incendiary bomb, weighing from 50 – 100 kg. and consisting of a thin steel case containing a mixture of crude oil and naphtha. Because of their resemblance to the 250 kg. and 500 kg. high explosive bombs, they were designated 'flam 250' and 'flam 500' according to size. They were detonated by a 1 kg. or 3 kg. charge of T.N.T. The intention was that burning oil should be scattered over a wide area but in practice these bombs often failed to ignite.

On the following night, Monday 9th September, there was bombing in the Haydons Road and Plough Lane area, a few minutes before midnight. An off licence at No.308 Haydons Road received a direct hit and seven people were killed. Among those who died was a young couple who were due to be married the following Saturday. No.4 and 4a Haydons Road were both seriously damaged and had to be demolished and another bomb fell in Cromwell Mews, at the rear of Haydons Road. There were no casualties from either of these incidents. Two bombs fell in Plough Lane, causing craters in the middle of the road, near the junction with Durnsford Road, and nearby houses were hit by blast and bomb splinters. Several other bombs fell on or near the railway tracks and in a garden at the rear of houses in Queens Road but these failed to explode.

The Royal Engineers dealt with unexploded bombs, except in the case of parachute mines, which were handled by the Royal Navy. However, it was found that there were so many reports of suspected unexploded bombs that a great deal of time was wasted in investigating false alarms. It was decided, therefore, to form a corps of reconnaissance officers who were trained to recognise and identify unexploded and delayed action bombs. In Wimbledon two wardens were trained as QRCD officers (Qualified Reconnaissance Civil Defence) and one policeman, at Inspector level, was trained as a QRP (Qualified Reconnaissance Police). The training course was very thorough, covering all types of missile likely to be encountered under air raid conditions and the training period extended over thirteen weeks. Part of the training was undertaken at army depots and practical exercises were carried out on bomb damage sites, where simulated incidents were arranged. Refresher courses were held every six months in order to keep up with the new types of weapons being introduced. As bombs penetrated to considerable depth it was necessary to be able to identify them from small pieces of debris, or even from particles of paint left on the surface. The two wardens who were trained for these duties were Mr. Ball, the Chief Warden, and Mr. Polak, a District Warden.

On 10th September there were five alerts and during the night bombs fell around White Cottage on Wimbledon Common and in filter beds at Durnsford Road. A delayed action bomb that fell in Wandsworth damaged some houses in Haslemere Avenue and Dawlish Avenue when it exploded. On 11th September there were four alerts and during the night raid, which lasted from 8.30 pm to 5.30 am, a number of incendiary bombs fell on Wimbledon Common.

Anti-aircraft fire had been exceptionally heavy during this raid. A pair of 5 inch guns was sited in a camp near the Windmill and a heavy gun mounted on a railway truck was used from sidings at Wimbledon Station but most of the noise came from rapid firing Bofors guns. These were mobile, rapid firing anti-aircraft guns and were set up in open spaces or even in streets in residential areas. The sound of artillery outside your front door could be unnerving. The bursting shells produced a shower of steel splinters, up to 0.5 kg. (1lb) in weight, which in a heavy barrage fell like hailstones. Children would collect them the following morning to take to school. Several small pieces could be swapped for one larger one and the brass nose cones were especially prized. On playing fields where rugby football was played, the teams would line up across the pitch and search for shell splinters before the game started. The game itself was considered dangerous enough without running the risk of being tackled and falling onto a jagged piece of steel.

Shell and bomb splinters also caused problems for Richmond Golf Club who had to introduce new rules:

RICHMOND GOLF CLUB

TEMPORARY RULES 1940

1. Players are asked to collect Bomb and Shrapnel splinters to save these causing damage to the mowing machines.

2. In Competitions, during gunfire or while bombs are falling, players may take cover without penalty for ceasing play.

3.   The positions of known delayed action bombs are marked by red flags at a reasonably, but not guaranteed, safe distance therefrom.

4.   Shrapnel and/or bomb splinters on the Fairway, or in Bunkers within a club's length of a ball, may be moved without penalty, and no penalty shall be incurred if a ball is thereby caused to move accidentally.

5.   A ball moved by enemy action may be replaced, or if lost or destroyed, a ball may be dropped not nearer the hole without penalty.

6.   A ball lying in a crater may be lifted and dropped not nearer the hole, preserving the line to the hole, without penalty.

7.   A player whose stroke is affected by the simultaneous explosion of a bomb may play another ball from the same place. Penalty, one stroke.

Sometimes shells failed to explode in the air and returned to earth, exploding on impact. Shell damage was particularly bad on the night of 11th September. No.40 and 42 Marlborough Road were hit and another shell landed on No.32 Wolseley Avenue, starting a small fire. Shells also hit the Horse & Groom public house in Haydons Road and the County School for Girls in Merton Hall Road. Others fell in the roadway at Wycliffe Road and at the corner of Haydons Road and South Road but these caused little damage.

The following night there was less anti-aircraft fire and fewer incidents. A bomb fell in Arthur Road, opposite No.38 (numbering in Arthur Road has since changed), causing a crater and fracturing gas and water mains and another fell nearby at No.25 Home Park Road. In Crescent Gardens a bomb fell outside No.33 and again a water main and electric mains were damaged. Representatives of the Gas Board, Electricity Board and Water Board had to be called out to make emergency repairs. In this type of incident they often had to work in dangerous and difficult conditions but their work was essential, not only to maintain services, particularly water pressure for the Fire Brigade, but to prevent the flooding of basement shelters. Where casualties were buried in the wreckage of houses, it was also important to protect the victims and rescuers from the effects of escaping gas. Because of the blackout they often had to work in total darkness, except of course where a gas main had been set on fire, which was not necessarily an advantage. In one incident a team working in the middle of the road had a member of the Messenger Service land on them, complete with bicycle, having failed to see the crater in the darkness. Other bombs that night fell in the filter beds at Durnsford Road, near the Wandsworth boundary, and in a playing field near the school in Havana Road. One that landed on the tennis courts adjoining the Woodman Hotel, Durnsford Road, failed to explode.

During the raid on the night of 13th September no bombs fell in Wimbledon but anti-aircraft fire was again heavy and a number of shells caused damage and casualties. The road junction of South Road and Haydons Road was hit again and another shell fell in St. George's Road opposite the Drill Hall. Two members of the Home Guard who were on duty at the hall were severely injured and died the following day in Wimbledon Hospital. At the top of Wimbledon Hill a shell landed at the junction with Ridgway and a fire was started at the Wimbledon Motor Works showroom. Two shells fell on Wimbledon Station, one landing on the railway tracks, the other on platform 1. Shells also fell in gardens of houses in Victory Road, near All Saints School, and in Grove Road. The damage resulting from anti-aircraft fire may have been greater than that caused to the enemy. Although some anti-aircraft guns did bring down enemy aircraft their chances of scoring a direct hit were very slight. Unlike German anti-aircraft guns that were radar controlled, our guns relied upon searchlights to pick out their targets. The gunners then had to estimate the height in order to get a shell anywhere near the aircraft. However, by September it was realised that the searchlights were more helpful in guiding German bombers to their targets than spotting them for our guns so from 10th September 1940 most of the searchlights were turned off and the anti-aircraft batteries around London were instructed to shoot blindly into the sky, at their maximum rate of fire. During that month 260,000 rounds of heavy anti-aircraft ammunition were used with little effect. However, the sound of gunfire was thought to boost the morale of the civilian population and did keep the German pilots at a high altitude. General Sir Frederick Pile, who commanded the AA defences, called it, "Not so much a barrage as a policy of despair."

Although the sirens sounded seven times on 14th September there were no incidents in Wimbledon but Sunday 15th September marked a turning point in the battle, although this was not realised until much later. The day began when a force of 300 German bombers, escorted by 500 fighters, attacked targets in south-east England. In July and August these raids would have been spread over a wide area, leaving Fighter Command guessing where the next attack would be. Daylight raids were concentrated on airfields and on factories involved with aircraft production. When residential districts were hit it was usually the result of error or because bombers had been diverted from their intended targets and jettisoned their bombs over the nearest built-up area. As the majority of raids were directed against south-east England it was 11 Group of Fighter Command that suffered most from the attacks on their airfields and at the same time had to provide most of the defence. 12 Group, based to the north of the Thames and in East Anglia, were too far away to provide much support. When they were called upon to protect 11 Group's airfields their pilots were so frustrated at not being able to take part in the main action that they would often chase after stray bombers, leaving the airfields unprotected.

Under these circumstances 11 Group had had to be very economical with the use of its fighters, sending only a squadron or two to intercept even the largest raids. As Air Chief Marshall Dowding put it, "If you don't send more than twelve you can't lose more than twelve." There were other fighter squadrons in the west country and in the north but these could not be called upon, except to provide replacement pilots and aircraft, or those parts of the country would have been left undefended. Because so few aircraft were being deployed at one time Herman Goering was convinced that the RAF was down to its last few fighters. His bomber pilots were not so convinced. Although the opposition was light there were always some fighters ready to intercept them. This gave rise to their saying, "Here come the last dozen Spitfires again."

However, since 24th August London had become the main target and this gave the RAF three advantages. Firstly, it gave 11 Group time to repair its damaged airfields; secondly, instead of having to spread its available aircraft over the whole of the south-east it could now concentrate all its resources against a single attacking force; thirdly, because London was on the boundary between 11 Group and 12 Group, it was possible to bring both these forces to bear on a single target. Now the RAF could put as many as 300 fighters into the air at one time and the Germans did not know what had hit them.

On 15th September there were many alerts and the sounds of aircraft and machine-gun fire continued throughout the day. Towards evening reports of heavy German losses began to circulate. Figures of 100, 150 and then 180 German planes destroyed were quoted against British losses of only 26 aircraft. At RAF Hornchurch the figure of 186 was written on the wall beside the telephone in the control tower and remained there until the building was demolished in 1966. Morale was high and when these figures were announced in public shelters crowds of people ran out into the streets and danced. But the raids continued into the night with heavy anti-aircraft fire and bombs falling in various parts of Wimbledon. Bombs hit No.80 and 89 Gladstone Road and another fell on the footpath outside No.3 Palmerston Road. Two shops at the corner of Wimbledon Broadway and Stanley Road were demolished, No.22 South Park Road was badly damaged and a crater was formed in the footpath in Princes Road. In Effra Road a bomb fell outside No.2 and a shell fell at the Haydons Road end. Three shops in Haydons Road, No.300 to 304, were destroyed while in Durnsford Road No.2 and 4 were demolished and No.6 and 8 badly damaged. An electricity sub-station was blown up and the entrance to the public shelter was wrecked, with debris halfway across Durnsford Road.

Mr. J.H. Young, an air raid warden, who was in Haydons Road at the time the bombs fell, made his way into the ruins of No.300, which had been a baker's shop. In the kitchen at the rear he found a woman who was buried in rubble so that only the top of her head and one arm were showing. He called in a rescue team and helped them to dig the woman out, but she was only half uncovered when another bomb fell nearby causing more of the building to collapse and burying her again. The team continued their rescue work although gas was escaping from broken pipes and the fires in the ovens of the demolished bake house were still burning. Mr. Young then went to the adjoining butcher's shop, where he believed two people were trapped, but as he was trying to get in, the front of the building collapsed and for a time it was thought that he had been buried. However, he had already moved on to the third shop and was helping people out of the wreckage. There was a strong concentration of gas in this building and the fumes overcame him. When he had recovered he found his way to nearby Cromwell Road where a delayed action bomb had hit No.11. He helped rescue an injured woman and then discovered eight people trapped under a staircase in the adjoining house. He brought them out and then started checking adjoining houses. While he was doing this the delayed action bomb exploded demolishing No.11, 13 and 15. At the rear of these buildings he found an air raid shelter partly buried in rubble and from this he rescued two more women. In recognition of his work on the night of 15th September Mr. Young was awarded the George Medal.

On the same night, No.43 to 47 Evelyn Road were destroyed and No.40 to 54 badly damaged. In Queens Road No.167 was hit but another bomb that fell at the rear of No.81 Cromwell Road failed to explode and was later removed. The south-west corner of Wimbledon Football Ground received a direct hit and No.6 Haydons Road was badly damaged. Bombs also fell at the rear of St. Mary's School, Russell Road and at the rear of No.1 and 3 Faraday Road but without serious effect. An anti-aircraft shell that fell through the roof of the Civic Hall exploded within the building, just after a dance had finished. Another exploded in the foyer of the King's Cinema in Wimbledon Broadway and a third fell near the station, outside the South Western Hotel. Two other shells failed to explode, one at No.78 Merton High Street and another on Wimbledon Common near the end of Lauriston Road. In this raid ten people were killed and eight seriously injured.

The significance of the events of 15th September was not realised until many years later. The figures for German losses on this day were actually lower than supposed at the time. They had lost only 60 of their force of 900 aircraft but their total losses since the middle of August had now reached more than 700 and the RAF seemed to be as strong as ever. In fact, the RAF had lost about 500 aircraft and although aircraft production had made good these losses there was a grave shortage of experienced pilots. From the German point of view it was the fact that they had not gained undisputed control of the air that was their problem. The normal process of blitzkrieg had failed and there was no way they could launch an invasion without control of the air. A few days later Operation Sealion, the planned invasion of England, was cancelled indefinitely.

The 15th September 1940 marked the end of what we now call the Battle of Britain. The young pilots of the RAF, some with only the minimum of training and experience, had managed to withstand the massive onslaught of the German Luftwaffe. However, to achieve this success it had been necessary to use every available aircraft in Fighter Command while the Germans had used only three of their five Air Fleets. Luftflotte 2, based in Belgium, Luftflotte 3, based in Northern France and the much smaller Luftflotte 5, based in Norway. The other two German Air Fleets, Luftflotte 1 and Luftflotte 4, had not even been called upon to make a contribution and had remained in Germany.

Mother and child. The civilian gas mask, designed to protect against various forms of poison gas, had a filter made from asbestos fibre!

41

The Wimbledon Tyre Company, at the corner of Kingston Road and Montague Road, received a direct hit in the first air raid on 16th August 1940.

The Ladies of Wimbledon, wearing Civil Defence type gasmasks, waiting to enter the decontamination centre at Queens Road school.

Ambulance crews at the Durham Road ambulance station.

Stretcher bearers in Worple Road.

Houses in Gladstone Road damaged on 15th September 1940.

Shops at the corner of Stanley road and The Broadway damaged in an air raid on the night of 15th September 1940.

Shops in The Broadway, adjoining those shown above, were damaged in a subsequent air raid on the night of 24th September 1940.

No. 33 Crescent Gardens was damaged during a raid on the night of 12th September 1940.

Houses in Revelstoke Road were damaged in a raid on the night of 19th September 1940.

A direct hit destroyed several houses in Melrose Avenue on the night of 19th September 1940.

No. 32 to 48 Glendale Drive were hit on the night of 11th October 1940 but an oil bomb that fell shortly afterwards failed to ignite.

THE BOMBS

The high explosive bombs used by the Germans in their air attacks were of two main types: general purpose and semi-armour-piercing. Fully armour-piercing bombs were hardly ever used on land targets and approximately 80% of all bombs dropped in the London area were of the general purpose (G.P.) type. The G.P. bomb had a comparatively thin tubular case of 6mm to 18mm thickness (¼" to ¾"). However, the nose of the bomb, which was a casting, was up to 125mm (5") at the point. The thin case allowed a large amount of explosive to be used in proportion to the weight of steel so that the explosive charge represented about 45% of the bomb's total weight. These bombs were cheaper to produce than the semi-armour-piercing type, which had a thick case of cast or forged steel. They were also less accurate but in the blanket bombing of built-up areas accuracy was not very important and the greater explosive charge and wider blasting power of the G.P. bomb was a positive advantage. The semi-armour-piercing bomb, with a case thickness of 25mm to 32mm (1" to 1¼") increasing to as much as 350mm (14") of solid steel at the nose, was designed to penetrate before exploding. Due to the thickness of the case, the explosive charge represented only 25% - 35% of the total weight.

During the 1940 Blitz the majority of bombs were of the 50 kg. (110 lb.), 250 kg. (550 lb.) or 500 kg. (1,100 lb.) G.P. type. 'A thousand pounder' was a term that came to be used by many people when referring to a large bomb but in fact by 1941 the size of bombs in common use had increased considerably. The 'Herman' 1,000 kg. (2,200 lb.) G.P. bomb was frequently used and the largest of the G.P. bombs, known as the 'Satan', made its appearance at this time. The bomb, which was the equivalent of the British 'Blockbuster', had an overall length of 3.75m (12' 4"), a diameter of 660mm (26") and a weight of 1,800 kg. (4,000 lb.). It could produce a crater that would accommodate several double-decker buses.

Another weapon that caused tremendous devastation was the parachute mine, or as it was sometimes known, the land mine. The mine was in fact identical to the magnetic mine used at sea and its effect on land targets may only have been realised after a number of these had fallen by accident on coastal towns. The Germans had a surplus of mines and converted many of them to land use by means of a time fuse in place of the magnetic trigger. Some were also fitted with acoustic fuses. It was said that hitting an acoustic fuse with a shovel would disabled it but it would take considerable nerve to test this theory. The mine was 600 mm (2' 0") diameter and 2.4m to 3m (8' 0"-10' 0") long, weighing about 1,000 kg. The steel casing was quite thin and the mine had to be dropped by parachute to prevent it breaking up on impact. The fuse ran for fifteen seconds after the mine landed and because it did not penetrate into the ground, blast damage was much more widely spread than with a conventional bomb.

Approximately 10% of all bombs dropped failed to explode. In Wimbledon out of a total of four hundred bombs, forty-eight did not explode on impact or, in a few cases, were rendered harmless before their delayed action mechanism could operate. This may seem a very high failure rate but it should be remembered that a bomb spends most of its life in a factory, an ammunition store or in the bomb bay of an aircraft. It is only in the last few seconds of its life that it is required to be sensitive. It is much more important that it should be safe and insensitive to heat, cold and physical shock during its manufacture, storage and transport than that it should be a hundred per cent efficient in use.

The explosive most commonly used in bombs was TNT, an explosive which although powerful was comparatively inert. It was poured into the bomb case in a molten state where it set into a solid block and required a considerable shock from a powerful priming charge to explode it. If ignited by heat it would burn with a fierce flame but would not explode and this method was used to dispose of unexploded bombs at the 'bomb cemetery', which was set up in Richmond Park. The Germans, on the other hand, often melted the explosive out of British bombs and re-used it in their own. Explosives were in short supply in Germany and in some of the larger bombs, particularly the 'Herman', TNT was used only in the nose section and the remainder of the case was filled with a cheaper explosive such as aluminized powder. Unexploded bombs of this type became unstable if they were left in the ground for any length of time as the two explosives reacted to produce nitro-glycerine. Later in the war explosives such as Amatol and RDX were used.

Apart from those bombs that failed to explode due to a mechanical or electrical fault, delayed action fuses were used from the earliest raids. These bombs often caused more trouble than those that exploded. Buildings had to be evacuated until the bomb had been removed or rendered safe and, where one fell in an industrial area, it could result in factories being closed down for several days. The attitude to bomb disposal at the beginning of the war was remarkably naive. It was supposed that bombs would remain on or near the surface and could easily be removed. However, it was soon found that in soft earth a small bomb would penetrate to a depth of 6m (20' 0") and a large bomb could reach a depth of 9m (30' 0") or more, often changing direction on the way down.

Bomb disposal units were formed and trained by the Royal Engineers and from the few bombs that had already fallen and from the details of the bomb fuses (which had been deposited by the Germans at the Patent Office some years before the war) they were able to build up a picture of the workings of the standard range of fuses. It was a common misconception that bombs were exploded by impact on a detonator in the nose. The standard form of fuse used by the Germans was electrical and was positioned halfway along the bomb in a tube, which ran through it from side to side. This tube contained the primer, composed of solid picric acid, and into this fitted the fuse with its detonator. The basic type 15 fuse contained a condenser capable of holding an electric charge for several days but it was not charged until the moment when the bomb left the aircraft. The fuse could be adapted to explode on impact or after a short predetermined delay. With the early fuses it was possible to discharge the condenser of an unexploded bomb by shorting it through the terminals by which it had been charged. However, more sophisticated fuses were soon introduced. The type 17 fuse had a time clock, inserted between the electrical fuse and the detonator, enabling delays of up to eighty hours to be set and this clock would continue to run even though the condenser had been discharged. The clock was only the size of a wristwatch and its ticking could only be detected using an electrical stethoscope. Sometimes the clock would stop of its own accord just before the bomb was due to explode. The slightest movement could cause it to start again even after many months in the ground. The whole fuse could be removed by unscrewing it, assuming of course that the bomb could be excavated before the delay had expired. So to prevent this being done the Germans fitted a mechanical booby trap (ZUS 40) behind it. For a time this problem was overcome by firing the bolt of a humane killer into the fuse to smash the clock mechanism but the Germans then countered this by introducing an explosive charge in front of the clock as well. We now know that this was coincidence but at that time a bomb disposal officer must have felt that there was always a German spy looking over his shoulder.

Much of the experimental work on dealing with bomb fuses was carried out in Richmond Park and the bombs were then rendered harmless or destroyed as necessary. One method adopted to overcome the fuse problem was to cut an opening in the bomb casing and to melt out the main charge of explosive by means of steam. The explosive was then stored in canvas bags waiting for disposal. One evening, when incendiary bombs fell in Richmond Park, a new recruit to the bomb disposal squad threw some of these bags onto the burning incendiaries thinking that they were sandbags.

The bomb disposal teams had to learn by trial and error and the errors were costing many lives. The number of unexploded bombs was far greater than expected and a system of priorities had to be introduced. Only bombs that affected vital industries or main communications were tackled immediately. In other built up areas, buildings were evacuated until the bombs had exploded. If there had been no explosion after ninety-six hours an attempt was made to remove the bomb or to explode it in situ. Bombs that fell on open land, such as Wimbledon Common, were left until there was time to deal with them. Some of them are probably still there. In spite of this system, the resources of the Engineers were insufficient to meet the demands on their time and by the end of August there were 2,500 unexploded bombs awaiting attention in the London area. By September the backlog had reached 3,750.

Delayed action fuses were normally used in bombs of 50 kg., 250 kg. or 500 kg.; hardly ever in the larger bombs. In 1941 a new fuse, the type 50, was introduced in the form of a battery-operated trembler. This fuse did not come into action until after the bomb had landed but then it became so sensitive that a pencil tapped on the bomb case could set off the detonator. In the 250 kg. and 500 kg. bombs two fuses were often fitted, one a time fuse, the other a trembler. A method of stopping the time fuses had now been devised which used powerful electro-magnets but the magnets could actuate the adjoining trembler fuse. A new way of stopping the clock was now found which consisted of injecting a sugar solution into the fuse. This clogged the clock and also slowed down the action of the mechanical booby trap. A solution of dental impression powder was found to be even better.

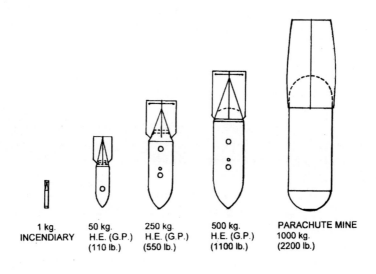

| 1 kg.
INCENDIARY | 50 kg.
H.E. (G.P.)
(110 lb.) | 250 kg.
H.E. (G.P.)
(550 lb.) | 500 kg.
H.E. (G.P.)
(1100 lb.) | PARACHUTE MINE
1000 kg.
(2200 lb.) |

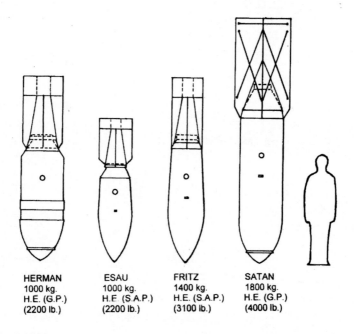

| HERMAN
1000 kg.
H.E. (G.P.)
(2200 lb.) | ESAU
1000 kg.
H.E. (S.A.P.)
(2200 lb.) | FRITZ
1400 kg.
H.E. (S.A.P.)
(3100 lb.) | SATAN
1800 kg.
H.E. (G.P.)
(4000 lb.) |

The comparative sizes of bombs used in the raids of 1940–1944

53

However, these solutions could not be used on the new trembler fuse as the liquid would cause a short circuit that would explode the bomb. A new complication was caused by the introduction of the type Y fuse. In this the initial charge from the condenser would activate a second circuit containing a dry battery. This enabled the fuse to remain active for up to a year. The only way to de-activate the battery was to freeze it. A ring of plasticine was formed around the fuse to provide a reservoir into which liquid oxygen could be poured. As it evaporated more liquid oxygen had to be added until at last a large ring of frost had formed on the surface of the bomb. This indicated that the freezing process had penetrated far enough to de-activate the battery but the fuse now had to be removed before the battery thawed out again. Sometimes carbon dioxide snow was used with methylated spirit. In either case it was a long process and the gasses released by evaporation could overcome the bomb disposal officer who would usually be working in a confined space.

Children playing on defused bombs on Wimbledon Common (Alan Bowles)

The oil and petrol bombs used in the early raids have already been described but by far the most frequent cause of fire was the 1 kg. incendiary bomb, of which several thousand fell in Wimbledon. This was much smaller than the oil bomb but more efficient. It consisted of a

54

thick tube of magnesium alloy, 50mm (2") diameter and 225mm (9") long. At the nose was a heavy steel cap containing the detonator, which fired on impact, and a tail assembly of three small steel fins completed the bomb. The incendiaries were dropped in canisters, containing thirty-six, which burst open above the ground scattering the bombs over a wide area. The filling used in these bombs was thermite, a mixture of powdered aluminium and iron oxide, which would burn without an external air supply and reach a temperature of nearly 3,000° C. The thermite mixture burnt for only one minute but the intense heat was sufficient to melt the magnesium case and throw particles of burning metal up to fifty feet. The magnesium then continued to burn for a further ten minutes.

The initial fire was so intense that it was difficult to smother and water sprayed directly onto a bomb would increase the blaze. A direct jet of water could cause it to explode. The method of dealing with incendiaries was to cover them with earth or sandbags and, if they were in a building, to spray the surrounding area with water to prevent the fire spreading. Once the initial blaze had died down the bombs were easy to smother or damp down.

Documentary films, shown at local cinemas, told householders how to deal quickly and efficiently with these incendiaries but in 1941 a new hazard was introduced when booby traps were added. These consisted of a small explosive charge fitted into the tail fin of the bomb in place of the normal filling plug. The charge exploded about one to one and a half minutes after the bomb had ignited. Towards the end of 1942 larger explosive charges were fitted to these bombs in the form of a nose cap 180mm (7½") long containing an explosive and fitted with a one to six minute time fuse. This considerably increased the weight of the bomb and gave it greater penetration so that it would often fall through the roof and top storey of a building before it started to burn.

Incendiary bombs were particularly effective when used in conjunction with high explosive bombs because they were more difficult to find and more likely to start a fire in a wrecked building. The chandelier bomb was developed to take advantage of this fact and to mark targets during night raids. The bomb consisted of a canister, which burst in mid air, throwing out six lighted fire pots to illuminate the target. From the centre of these fell one high explosive bomb and sixty incendiaries.

Wimbledon was spared some of the more horrific weapons that were used in other towns, such as the 50 kg. phosphorous bomb, which contained a mixture of phosphorous, oil and rubber, and the sensitive anti-personnel butterfly bombs, but Wimbledon did not escape the flying bombs that arrived in droves during 1944. These, and the damage that they caused, are described in a later chapter.

A 'Satan', 1,800 kg. bomb, that fell near Camp Road and failed to explode. It was excavated from a depth of thirty feet.

THE BLITZ

From the middle of September 1940 the bombing policy of the Luftwaffe changed. Although daylight raids continued the main bomber force now concentrated on night raids. The repeated bombing of London and its suburbs came to be known as 'The Blitz' but this was a misnomer; there was nothing of the 'lightning strike' about the nightly bombing of London and its suburbs. The main targets were factories, warehouses, railways and docks but the policy behind the bombing was primarily to break the morale of the people. The air raids became more regular, with the main evening raid starting at about 9 p.m. and continuing until the early hours of the morning. A chart of the air raid alerts in Wimbledon during the autumn of 1940 shows that there were over three hundred alerts in a period of three months. As the days shortened the night raids grew longer, lasting for twelve or thirteen hours.

On 16th September 1940 there were six alerts in Wimbledon but only two incidents, when incendiary bombs caused minor fires, one at Merton Hall Road School and another at No.10 Cross Road. On 17th September there were several alerts during the day and at 8.25 pm a large bomb fell on the Lysol Chemical Works in Kingston Road causing extensive damage. A large crater blocked the road and water and gas mains were burst. A trench shelter belonging to the firm was hit and there were eight casualties. Houses over a wide area were damaged by the blast from this bomb and others suffered from bombs falling in the Merton area during the night.

The effects of bombing depended not only on the size and type of bomb but upon the location in which it fell. A bomb that hit a building and exploded above ground often produced damage over a wide area. Near to an explosion the outward blast would be followed by an inward suction as air rushed in to fill the void. In some cases the blast would lift the roof of an adjoining house and the unrestrained walls would be sucked outwards before the roof came crashing down. Beyond this the windows of surrounding houses would be blown in and the tiles or slates ripped from the roof. In those days, ceilings were nearly all of lath and plaster and these would collapse producing clouds of dust. Sometimes the plaster would just be loosened and not fall until several days or weeks later when the vibration from a distant explosion would bring it down onto residents who had thought their troubles were over.

When people were caught out in the open by the blast from a bomb they were usually killed outright without a mark being left on their bodies, although most if not all of their clothing would have disappeared. Bombs that fell in gardens or other open spaces often penetrated well into the ground before exploding and the blast was directed upwards. Although the bomb would form a large crater, surrounding houses might escape without even the loss of their windows.

There was considerable air activity on 18th September and many warnings. Local historian Richard Milward, who was living in West Wimbledon, kept a diary in which he recorded every air raid during this period. His entry for that day records the following events: "The all clear sounded at 5.55am. Sirens sounded again at 7.15 and German planes passed over. All clear followed at 7.32. Warning at 8.18. Heavy anti-aircraft fire, all clear sounded at 8.42. Sirens again at 9.37, many fighters passed over. All clear 10.20. Warning at 11.32 no action. All clear sounded ten minutes later. 12.44 pm warning sounded, saw twelve Hurricanes in pairs and singly. All clear sounded 2.26. Warning sounded 4.05 all quiet and all clear sounded at 4.22. Warning at 5.11 pm. Heard and saw many of our own fighters. All clear at 5.55. 7.55 pm warning followed by German planes, searchlights, very heavy anti-aircraft fire. Some shrapnel but above all many screaming bombs dropped nearby and some fire bombs."

The first bombs fell in Cambridge Road, between Panmuir Road and Laurel Road. One fell in the children's play area where underground shelters had been built, forming a large crater. There were no casualties in the shelters but the people were badly shaken and, as adjoining gas mains and water mains had been broken, it was decided to evacuate them to shelters in Holland Gardens. The bombs were of the 250 kg. size. It was known that these normally dropped in clusters of six and, as there had been only five explosions, a search was started for the missing bomb. The search had reached No.127 Durham Road when the bomb, which had landed in the garden at the rear, exploded. A cluster of bombs fell around King's College School and one hit the chlorination plant at the side of the swimming pool. Another landed on the tennis courts and three more fell in the garden of the headmaster's house at 7 Woodhayes Road (now Peregrine Way).

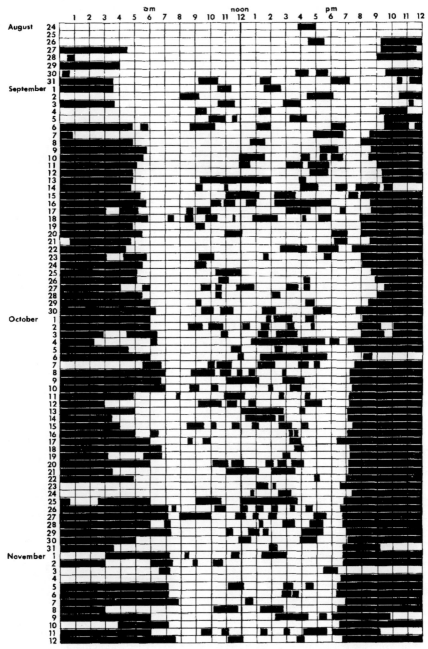

Air raid alerts in Wimbledon in the autumn of 1940

59

Mr. Arthur Webb contemplating the remains of his house at 127 Durham Road following the explosion of a delayed action bomb on 19th September 1940.

In Alexandra Road, No.58 was burnt out by a petrol bomb and a fire was started at No.92 by a similar bomb. These bombs were basically the same as the oil bombs previously described but tended to burn more fiercely and for a shorter period.

Springfield Court, in Springfield Road, was hit by a high explosive bomb, which demolished most of the block of four flats and damaged the gas main. Another fell in the east sidings of the railway adjoining Alexandra Road. On Wimbledon Common, a large crater was formed between North View and White Cottage and a bomb fell on open land at the rear of No.5 Leopold Avenue. Small fires were started by incendiaries in the car park at Wimbledon Stadium, in Wandle Park and in Grove Road. Remarkably, there were only three casualties from all these incidents.

Thursday 19th September was a comparatively quiet day. Bombing did not start until nearly 11.0 pm. The first bombs fell in the north-east of the borough at Melrose Avenue. Extensive damage was caused between Ashen Grove and Revelstoke Road by two large high explosive bombs that landed in the road. No.85 to 91 and 108 to 112 were completely destroyed and other houses adjoining and on the opposite side of the road sustained serious damage. Gas, water mains and sewers were broken and No.5 in the same road was set on fire by an incendiary bomb. A bomb that fell at the rear of No.18 Albany Road wrecked No.14 to 18. In Queens Road another fell at the junction with Craven Gardens, causing only minor damage to the buildings but creating a large crater in the road and breaking the mains. The first person to arrive on the scene of this incident was picking his way through the rubble with the aid of a torch when a warden shouted at him to "douse the light", ignoring the fact that the gas main was now burning with a flame twenty feet high.

Nearby in Faraday Road more houses were wrecked by high explosive bombs, which fell between Evelyn Road and Birkbeck Road. No.89 to 97 and No.78 were destroyed. In Home Park Road a bomb fell in the garden at the rear of No.80 but caused little damage. At the corner of Cromwell Road and Avondale Road blast damage was caused to adjoining buildings by a bomb that landed on the pavement.

The anti-aircraft fire was exceptionally heavy that night and 20 minutes after midnight a German plane was hit over London and dived steeply towards Wimbledon. The aircraft was a Junkers 88 (No.4148

61

from II Gruppe, Kampfgeschwader 54) and it left behind it a trail of burning fragments. Part of a turret, complete with machine gun, fell in the grounds of Woodside House and a flying helmet was found in Gap Road. The pilot and two other members of the crew were killed but the gunner, Fw. Schlake, managed to bale out. In a letter written to a Wimbledon resident after the war he said that at the time the aircraft was hit he was not wearing his parachute and had great difficulty in finding it. When at last he did manage to escape he found himself suspended in pouring rain and recognised the tower of Big Ben immediately below him. However, the wind carried him south and he eventually landed on the roof of a house in Clapham. Having climbed down he entered the house and, although armed, surrendered to the family who were sheltering in the cellar. The aircraft flew on, skimming over the rooftops and eventually crashed into No.2 and 4 Richmond Avenue, Merton, close to the Nelson Hospital. It was carrying 1,000 kg. bombs but fortunately these did not explode on impact. Patients from the hospital were evacuated to the nearby Merton Park Studios, right next to the film vaults containing rolls of nitro-cellulose film!

Although the sirens sounded again the following day there were no incidents in Wimbledon but on the night of 21st September there was a fire raid. Only one high explosive bomb fell and this was on open ground at the junction of Hood Road and Beverley Avenue but many hundreds of incendiary bombs were released in an area roughly between Cottenham Park recreation ground and Wimbledon Common. Many failed to ignite but the top floors of several houses were severely damaged by fire and others were slightly damaged. Wardens dealt with most of the bombs but in a few cases, where the fires were out of hand, the fire brigade had to be called. Among the houses damaged by fire that night were Oakfield in Somerset Road, Uplands in Oakfield Road, Oakhurst in Bathgate Road and No.7 Woodhayes Road. The following morning King's College boys, on their way to school, could be seen kneeling down in the grass at the edge of the Common pulling unexploded incendiaries out of the ground by their tail fins. You could get an awful lot of shell splinters in exchange for one unexploded incendiary bomb!

During 22nd and 23rd September the air raid warning sounded seven times but there were no incidents in Wimbledon. On the night of Tuesday 24th September bombs fell again in the area of Wimbledon Broadway and South Park Road.   No.124 to 126 the Broadway received a direct hit and these buildings were destroyed, together with No.128 and 130. No.132 and 134 at the corner of Stanley Road had already been wrecked by the raid of 15th September. All the shops in the Broadway, from No.120 to 140 and from 117 to 133, were badly damaged. (This group of shops, with offices over, was among the first to be rebuilt after the war and have since been rebuilt again.)

The Broadway was blocked with rubble mixed with groceries, bicycle parts and furniture blown from the wrecked shops. On top of the pile stood the plaster bust, complete with wig and a Gainsborough hat, that had stood in the window of the hairdressers. Alderman Hickmott was, as usual, in the control room when the incident was reported. He owned three of the shops.

A bomb that exploded in the cellar of a bakery on the other side of the road also damaged the front of the Baptist Chapel on the corner of Palmerston Road. Ambulance workers who had to bring out an elderly couple from one of the buildings found the husband very agitated. He thought that his wife had been injured because she was quite unable to move. However, they found that in the darkness she had put both feet into one leg of her woollen combinations. Her husband, still agitated and trying to dress himself in the dark, managed to tuck the curtains into his trousers with his shirt and brought the heavy curtain rail crashing down.

A bomb that fell at the corner of South Park Gardens caused damage to No.1 to 17 Dudley Road and No.22 to 46 Kings Road. The nearby block of flats, Kings Court, was slightly damaged. A large crater blocked Dudley Road and gas mains in both roads were fractured. Shortly before 1.0 am further bombs fell in Wimbledon Park. One formed a crater about a hundred metres from the sports pavilion and another fell a few metres away but failed to explode. There were no casualties that night.

Day and night alerts continued but there were no further incidents until early in the morning of Friday 27th September when the South Park Road, Kings Road area was again hit. No.12a, 14 and 16 South Park Road were reduced to rubble and No.39 to 49 were badly damaged. A high explosive bomb in Princes Road, between Kings Road and Stanley Road, destroyed No.18 to 22 and four people were killed. A number of incendiaries fell in the Wandle/Leyton Road area but the majority of these bombs fell in gardens and all fires were put out without much damage being caused. Extensive damage in Garfield Road and Haydons Road resulted from bombs that fell in the Merton and Morden area.

There were another five air raid warnings on 27th September and in the early hours of Saturday 28th there were further incidents. There had been four warnings during the day and at 8.19 pm the raiders returned. A bomb that fell outside No.105 Worple Road caused substantial damage to adjoining houses. Gas and water mains and electricity cables were broken and Worple Road was blown open for half its width. Ambulances found difficulty in driving through the tangle of trolleybus wires that had been brought down by the explosion. In Copse Hill an oil bomb landed close to Christ Church and another fell in the garden of Holmehurst nearby, causing a fire in an outbuilding and slight damage to the house. A bomb that fell in the playing fields of Rokeby School in The Downs failed to explode. On the other side of Wimbledon a bomb fell in Haslemere Avenue, completely blocking the road, fracturing the sewer and gas main. No.8, 10 and 12 were badly damaged and the front of the Britannic Works was hit by blast. An oil bomb also fell in this road outside No.26 and 28 adding to the glare from the burning gas.

There were several more warnings but no further incidents in the next two days, apart from an anti-aircraft shell damaging the front of No.35 Dryden Road. On the night of 1st October bombs again fell in the Wimbledon Park area. Two fell on the golf course, one landing on the edge of the lake causing very little damage, but the bomb that hit No. 85 Home Park Road demolished the house and No.83 and 87 were severely damaged. Two women were trapped in the ruins of No.85. One was rescued but the other was completely buried under the debris and was only traced by her cries. Fortunately the telephone in the adjoining house was still working and Bill Myson, who was the incident officer, was able to organise rescue operations with the least possible delay by obtaining a priority line to the Control Centre. The whole building had collapsed into a pile of masonry and timber and it was difficult for the rescuers to know where to dig. Mr. F.J. Gradden, Deputy Leader of the Rescue Squad, managed to find an opening in the rubble and proceeded to dig a tunnel towards the estimated position of the victim. It took him two and a half hours, cutting through timber and rubble, to form a tunnel twenty feet long. He found the woman but she was completely trapped and unable to move head or limbs. It was decided to dig down vertically to reach her and Mr. Gradden was ordered to leave the tunnel

64

because of the danger of collapsing masonry. Some of the blocks above him were estimated to weigh up to half a tonne and the debris was now becoming impregnated with gas. However, he refused to leave the woman and remained with her, guiding the diggers above, for a further three and a half hours. She was rescued at 8.30 am the following morning and was taken to hospital with minor injuries. Mr. Gradden was awarded the George Medal for his part in the rescue.

On the 2nd and 3rd October there were fourteen periods of alert but no incidents. By now people were using their own judgment about when to take shelter. For example, if factory workers had left their workbenches every time the sirens sounded little work would have been done. Instead most industrial premises now had observation posts on their roofs and the workers only made a dash for the shelters when aircraft were actually seen to be approaching.

On the night of Friday 4th October at 10.15 pm bombs fell in Arthur Road. One was in the garden at the rear of No.41 and another at the front of 45. Neither caused serious damage. Incendiaries fell in the Durnsford Road recreation ground and on the banks of the Southern Railway adjoining but these were soon extinguished. The raids on 6th and 7th October produced no incidents, other than an oil bomb that fell in a meadow on the south side of Barham Road. One high explosive and one oil bomb fell just before midnight on 8th October on the Royal Wimbledon golf course adjacent to Ellerton Road and four houses were damaged but there were no casualties.

Wednesday 9th October was a comparatively quiet night although the raid was one of the longest so far, lasting for nearly twelve hours. Bombs falling in Wandsworth damaged some houses in Bathgate Road and Queensmere Road. In contrast, the raid on the night of 10th October was very concentrated and the anti-aircraft fire was exceptionally heavy. The bombing occurred in the short period between 9.50 pm and 10.03 pm. High explosive bombs fell at the rear of No.20 Haydon Park Road, destroying No.18 to 26 and causing damage to No.15 to 19 Cromwell Road. About forty incendiaries fell in the Revelstoke Road, Braemar Avenue area and a shell fell in Tennyson Road. The major incident of the night was caused by a parachute mine that fell at the rear of houses in Russell Road, near the Broadway. No.28 to 42 were demolished and all houses from No.20 to 44 were seriously damaged. Houses in Palmerston Road were also affected. St. Mary's School was wrecked and houses on the opposite side of the road were hit by the blast. Many houses in Pelham Road, the Broadway and Gladstone Road were also damaged. Seven people were killed and thirty-three injured, nine of them seriously. An Anderson shelter was crushed by the blast and the wreckage was still being searched for casualties during most of the following day. It was not always possible to differentiate between damage caused by a parachute mine and a large bomb of the conventional type but in this case the aircraft had been caught in searchlights and the mine was seen to leave the aircraft and descend on its parachute. The messenger who saw this happening above him is said to have broken all cycling records.

The following day, Friday 11th October, was quiet but at night the bombers returned and between 11.0 pm and midnight high explosive, oil and incendiary bombs fell in Wimbledon. The first bomb of the evening was in Florence Road, between Ashley Road and Edith Road, demolishing No.142 to 152. The road was completely blocked by a crater and all services and mains were broken. Nearby, in Faraday Road, a bomb fell at the rear of No.87. This house had been damaged in a previous raid and the 'first aid' repairs had just been completed.

Temporary repairs had to be made as soon as possible to prevent buildings being further damaged by rain. Local builders were often called out in the early hours of the morning or late at night to throw tarpaulins over the roofs of houses where slates and tiles had been blown off. Where houses were still standing but no longer habitable, the furniture had to be taken away and put into storage. Window glass, when it was available, was of very poor quality. Emergency repairs usually consisted of bituminous felt nailed over the lower parts of windows and a waxed fabric, which allowed in a certain amount of light, nailed over the upper part. There was a great shortage of W.C. pans. These were often broken by blast and replacements were almost unobtainable. In the case of No.87 Faraday Road this was no problem; the second bomb destroyed the house completely, together with No.89 and 91. In Compton Road a bomb destroyed No.46 and 48 and caused serious damage to the adjoining houses; one of the casualties was a soldier home on leave. Telephone and electricity cables were severed.

In Glendale Drive, off Woodside, a bomb fell on a new block of maisonettes demolishing No.32 to 48 and causing considerable damage to other adjoining properties and to No.30 to 40 Bernard Gardens.

66

Shortly afterwards an oil bomb fell among the wreckage but fortunately it failed to ignite. The maisonettes were constructed with concrete floors and these collapsed one onto another. The rescue teams worked through the night and brought out five people who had been trapped. The following day extra rescue teams were brought in but it was several days before all the bodies had been recovered.

At the All England Lawn Tennis Club two bombs fell: the first near Church Road, blocking the road and breaking a large gas main, and the second fell near Somerset Road. A stick of four high explosive bombs fell in the Worple Road area between Arterberry Road and Langham Road: one outside No.143, two others in the gardens between Worple Road and Stanton Road and a fourth in the garden at the rear of No. 121. These caused extensive damage to all the houses at the western end of Worple Road and to No.54 to 60 Stanton Road. Of the four air raid wardens who were on patrol in the Worple Road area at the time three were seriously injured and one died. Two other people were killed and eighteen injured. In Haslemere Avenue a bomb hit the Ironclad Mantle factory, demolishing part of the main building. An oil bomb that fell at the same time landed in the river Wandle. Another oil bomb landed in the Council road depot at Queens Road but workmen put this out before it could cause any damage. Although there were five air raid warnings the following day, and some heavy gunfire during the night, there were no incidents on 12th October.

On Sunday 13th October there was more bombing and heavy casualty figures. The worst incident was at the United Dairies premises, adjoining Gap Road Bridge. A large bomb fell close to the air raid shelter, which was wrecked, trapping some twenty-three people and killing four. Another, which fell nearby at No.55 Gap Road, caused severe damage to No.52 to 57 and to the isolation hospital adjoining. Many people in Gap Road who were sheltering in basements were endangered by a very large water main that burst under Gap Road cemetery. Water flooded down the main path in waves, leaping like breakers on a beach. An attempt was made to build a dam from the large slabs of clay that had been blown out of the crater but fortunately a rise in the road near the main gates diverted the water sideways so that it formed a lake retained by the walls of the graveyard. The third bomb of this group fell in Cromwell Road, between No.62 and 64. The combined effect of these bombs was to cause extensive damage to properties in Ashcombe Road, Albany Road and the

Haydon Park Road areas. Altogether fourteen people, including one warden, were killed and seven injured. On Wimbledon Common a bomb fell close to The Bungalow, Cannizaro Park, killing one person and injuring another. An oil bomb, which fell at the same time, landed in the grounds of Westside House.

Worple Road was again hit on the night of 14th October. The raid started at 7.0 pm with many aircraft passing overhead and heavy gunfire. Shortly before midnight a bomb fell in the forecourt of No.27 Worple Road, destroying this and No.25. No.19 received a direct hit. Adjoining houses were wrecked and houses on the opposite side of the road and in Crescent Road and Arterberry Roads were damaged.

A woman who was being carried out of the wreckage of her house on a stretcher told her rescuers that there was a bottle of whisky for them in the sideboard in the dining room. Then she thought for a moment and added, "If you can find the sideboard — if you can find the dining room." A third bomb, which fell at the rear of No.194 Worple Road, destroyed No.192 and 194 and caused serious damage to No.190 and to houses in Delamere Road. There were four casualties, one killed and three injured. No.11 and 12 Railway Place received a direct hit, No.9 and 10 having been destroyed in an earlier raid. On Wimbledon Hill a bomb fell at the rear of No.98 and another wrecked the surface shelter on one of the lawns at Wimbledon High School but there were no casualties.

At the top of the hill a bomb fell at the rear of No.67 Murray Road and another fell in the grounds of Lauriston House nearby. In Oldfield Road a delayed action bomb landed at the rear of No.14. Adjoining houses were evacuated but the bomb did not explode until mid-day on the 15th October, when it destroyed No.14 and damaged a number of adjoining houses. A fire broke out but it was quickly brought under control. Several oil bombs also fell that night, landing in the gardens of No.12 Murray Road, 42 Marryat Road and 13 Dunmore Road. A fourth oil bomb landed in the grounds of the All England Lawn Tennis Club. These bombs detonated but did not ignite.

The sirens sounded seven times the next day and soon after the last warning at 7.28 pm further high explosive, oil and incendiary bombs fell. Worple Road was hit again, the first bomb forming a large crater outside No.6 near the junction with Cranbrook Road. The road was completely blocked, overhead trolley-bus wires were brought down and the gas main was broken.

68

At the Southern Railway power station in Durnsford Road a bomb fell straight down one of the two 280ft. (85m) chimney stacks, demolishing it but leaving the other standing. This was one of two stations providing power to the whole of the Southern Region and although the generators were not damaged, trains were reduced to half speed for more than a week.

An oil bomb landed in the grounds of Wimbledon High School, near Mansel Road, and another at the rear of Sussex House in Raymond Road. In Gladstone Road a high explosive bomb fell at the rear of No.62 and approximately one hundred incendiary bombs fell in the area of Wimbledon Park and South Park, including about forty on the Wimbledon Football Ground. Most of the fires resulting from these were small. The roof and upper floor of No.19 Vineyard Hill Road were badly damaged and there was internal damage to the Baptist Church Hall in Haydons Road. Six people were injured.

Dense cloud and heavy rain meant that there was very little activity on 16th October but on the 17th there were four alerts and shortly before midnight seven small high explosive bombs were dropped. Two fell on the Sunlight Laundry premises in York Road, two at the rear of No.49 South Park Road, and another two on the Southern Railway sheds off Durnsford Road. The last to fall was a direct hit on the front of a shop at No.56 Hartfield Road. No.41 Marryat Road was damaged that night by an anti-aircraft shell.

There were several alerts and some gunfire on the 18th but no further bombing. On the night of Saturday 19th October one high explosive bomb fell on the Southern Railway main line, east of Durnsford Road Bridge, derailing a train. Rescuers had to crawl through the wreckage in the dark trying to avoid the live rails. One person was killed and ten injured. The only other incident that night was an oil bomb that fell in Wellington Road. The next afternoon damage was caused to properties in Merton High Street and Leyton Road by bombs falling in the Merton area and at 10.20 pm bombs fell in Cambridge Road. The first fell at the rear of No.55, wrecking this and the adjoining houses. Another landed on the footpath, damaging a gas main, which caught fire.

Two more bombs fell by the trench shelters in Cottenham Park recreation ground, wrecking the wardens' post and damaging the entrance to one of the trenches. There was no panic in the shelters but

On the night of 19th October 1940 a bomb derailed this train near Durnsford Road Bridge.

it was decided that they should be evacuated for the night. These shelters still exist under the park although they have long since been covered over.

In the area of Ashen Grove and Braemar Avenue, widespread damage was caused by three bombs that destroyed approximately forty houses and two shops. No.15 to 19 Ashen Grove were reduced to rubble and No.8 to 14, which were badly damaged by the first bomb, were demolished by a delayed action bomb that exploded in the early hours of the morning. No.1 and 3 and 2 to 18 Ashen Grove were demolished and No.53 to 67 and 54 to 68 Braemar Avenue were wrecked, together with No.113 to 127 Revelstoke Road. Incendiary bombs fell again in the Haydons Road area, causing slight damage to St. Peter's Church, a timber yard in Effra Road and several houses. But all fires were soon under control except for a gas main, the flames from which could be seen over a mile away. It was estimated that some forty to fifty incendiaries were involved.

From all these incidents nine people were killed, twelve seriously injured and a further twenty-five slightly injured. One hundred and forty people were rendered homeless and were taken to the Central Hall shelter station. The police had a problem recording the deaths that occurred during this raid. It was difficult to know if there were casualties or bodies buried in the wreckage as it took several days to clear the debris and the records of owners and tenants often proved to be inaccurate.

Following these incidents it was decided that more information was required on the number of occupants in each house, so that rescue teams would know where to look for survivors and would not waste their time on houses that were empty. A survey was carried out by wardens making door to door enquiries and listing the names of people who would normally be in the house during the various times of day and night.

Only two bombs fell on the night of 21st October, one in Somerset Road by the All England Lawn Tennis Club, the other in the field opposite. The 22nd was another peaceful day but just before midnight another four small bombs fell in the Copse Hill area. A crater blocked the road outside No.132 Copse Hill and another bomb fell in the playing fields adjoining the Oberon First Aid Post in Lindisfarne Road. In Coombe Lane a bomb fell at the rear of No.236 and 238, both of which were badly damaged, and a fourth fell on Cottenham Park allotments. There were no incidents on the night of 23rd October, although gunfire could be heard in the distance.

Approximately one hundred and fifty incendiary bombs fell in the Haydons Road area on the night of the 24th. Most of them fell between South Road and Plough Lane and although many landed on open ground, about thirty fires were started. Three high explosive bombs fell on the common, near Camp Road, close to Caesar's Camp. Only one caused any serious damage when a forty-two inch water main was broken by a direct hit.

There was more activity on the night of 25th October with heavy anti-aircraft fire and a number of bombs. In Merton High Street, near the corner of Leyton Road, a large crater blocked the road and gas and water mains were broken. Pieces of tramline were hurled into the air and the overhead cables were brought down. No.40 to 44 Merton High Street were demolished but people in an Anderson shelter within a few yards of the crater were unharmed. A number of other buildings, including some houses in Leyton Road, were also damaged.

The Oberon first aid post at Lindisfarne Road was again shaken by a bomb that fell nearby. Other bombs fell in open spaces off the Kingston by-pass and in a field at the end of Preston Road, causing serious damage to No.7, 9 and 11 but an oil bomb that fell at Cottenham Park allotments did not ignite.

Saturday 26th October was a day of almost continuous alerts. Raids always seemed to be more numerous and more severe at weekends and on this day there were eight alerts. Gunfire was very heavy and although rubber earplugs had now been issued they were not very effective against the sharp crack of the Bofors guns.

Just before 10.0 pm bombs fell at the rear of No.11 and 13 Ridgway Place, demolishing both houses, and at the rear of No.74 and 76 Kenilworth Avenue. Both these houses were demolished and many others in the road were badly damaged. A bomb fell in open ground close to Johnson Ward at the isolation hospital in Gap Road, and patients from two wards were evacuated to another part of the hospital. A bomb, which fell at the rear of No.24 Arthur Road, failed to explode. Many incendiaries fell in the area of Cannizaro, Westside, and Atkinson Morley Hospital and minor damage was caused to No.8 Ernle Road and to No.32 Crooked Billet. In the last three days of October there were no further incidents, although the air-raid warnings sounded twenty-two times.

The first day of November brought with it an unfortunate accident. A delayed action bomb fell at about 7.30 pm between No.16 and 18 Burghley Road. It was a large bomb and the damage that it caused by falling was so great that it was thought to have exploded. The adjoining houses were not evacuated and at 2.30 the following morning the bomb exploded, killing two people and seriously injuring three others. Bombs also fell that night in Wyke Road, on the strip of land between the road and the railway, and at the junction of Montana Road and Arterberry Road, damaging water and gas mains. At Marryat Road one fell on the edge of the lake in the grounds of Margin House and an oil bomb fell between No.32 and 34 Burghley Road but it did not ignite. Three bombs that fell in a stick caused little damage. The first landed in the garden at the rear of No.145 Worple Road, the second at the rear of No.19 Crescent Road, and the third on the lawn at the rear of No.11 Lansdowne Road.

An anti-aircraft shell, falling onto the concrete path near No.8 Pitt Crescent, caused minor damage and another fell in the garden of No.40 Wolseley Avenue.

There were only a few warnings during the next two days and on the night of 3rd November sirens did not sound at all, the first time for fifty-nine nights. The following day, 4th November, there were no daylight raids either and this was the first time that the sirens had not sounded during the day since the raids had started in the middle of August.

Bomb damage in South Park Road.

THE SHELTERS

The regularity of the raids, night after night for months on end, created distinctive behaviour patterns in the civilian population. Those who were in the Civil Defence services and who had to be out in the open during the raids, learnt to recognise the differences between the sounds of various bombs and shells that represented an immediate and very real danger and the general background noise of gunfire and falling splinters that had to be accepted and ignored. Of those who did not have to venture out into the night, some slept in their own beds on the fatalistic principle that if a bomb 'had their name on it' they would be killed no matter where they were. One man must have had second thoughts about this when, returning to his bed after a brief absence, he found the nose cone of a shell buried in the pillow. Another man, living in South Park Road who had been sleeping in a ground floor room, found himself on the roof, unharmed except for bruises, when the front of the house was blown out.

For those with gardens, Anderson shelters offered good protection against blast, although they offered little protection against cold and damp. They were supplied free to people with incomes less than £250 p.a. and for others the price was £7. The Anderson shelter was constructed of heavy gauge corrugated steel sheet, vertical at the sides and curving over to meet at the top. The shelter was sunken 1m (3'.3") into the ground and covered with sandbags or soil. At each end there were more vertical sheets with a hole at ground level in one end to form an entrance and a removable panel in the other in case the entrance should become blocked. The internal dimensions were 1.5m x 2m (5'.0" x 6'.6") and 1.8m (6'.0") high. These shelters were designed to accommodate six people! The steel itself gave little protection against bomb splinters but the soil covering was very effective. The minimum thickness of soil recommended was 750mm. (30") at the sides and ends and 370mm (15") on top. The normal covering to the entrance was a piece of blanket but some people built a 'blast wall' of brick or concrete blocks a short distance in front of the opening. Many of these shelters survived almost direct hits from small bombs. Where large bombs were concerned, however, the shelters could be death traps. The blast from a 500 kg. or 1,000 kg. bomb was sometimes sufficient to flatten the shelter, crushing the people inside it.

An Anderson shelter gave good protection from blast but could not withstand a direct hit. Fortunately in this case the family had stayed in bed and survived.

It had been anticipated at the beginning of the war that air raids would be of short duration and shelters were designed on this principle. As the all night raids developed people attempted to make their shelters more comfortable. Bunk beds were built so that they could sleep, or attempt to sleep, in them. Heating became a problem as the winter progressed. Oil heaters produced fumes and condensation so a new form of heating was developed. A candle was placed inside a large flowerpot and then another flowerpot was placed upside down on top of it. The slight gap between the pots and the hole at the top allowed sufficient air to circulate to keep the candle alight. The flowerpots became surprisingly hot and radiated sufficient heat to keep the shelter above freezing point. Many people took some personal belongings with them when they went to the shelter because they did not know if their house would still be there when they came out again. Some took spare clothing, valuables or irreplaceable souvenirs but identity cards and ration books were the most important.

A family coming to terms with life below ground in a deep air raid shelter.

For those who took shelter outside the home there were various types of public shelter. In some minor roads brick built shelters were erected directly on the road surface. But although they could withstand a considerable amount of blast they were as vulnerable as houses to direct hits or near misses. Some buildings were reinforced to withstand blast and were used as surface shelters but these were similarly vulnerable. Part of the basement at the Town Hall was used as a public shelter and underground shelters were constructed in parks and school playgrounds. The underground shelters were much safer than those on the surface. They were formed of concrete arches, partly or completely below ground level, with an entrance that was approached by steps and screened by a concrete or brick blast wall. Timber slatted benches lined the walls and the floor was usually covered with duckboards because of the water that seeped through onto the floor. At the far end of each shelter was an escape hatch reached by means of a steel ladder. Some were provided with a chemical lavatory.

Many of the public shelters were quite unsuitable for the twelve-hour night raids that developed during the autumn and winter of 1940. As they became waterlogged by winter rains more and more people stayed in their own beds or took refuge in improvised shelters in their houses. Where there was a cellar this was the obvious place of refuge, although there was some danger from flooding or gas when the mains were fractured. From the observation of bomb damage to properties it was notable that one of the safest places to shelter was under a staircase. This space would only accommodate one or two people and would obviously offer no protection against a direct hit but in many cases where houses were severely damaged the staircase remained standing.

Residents in Arthur Road had an unusually historic air raid shelter dating back to about 1735. Wimbledon Park House still stood on the south side of Arthur Road, opposite the junction with Home Park Road, and from the basement of this house ran an arched brick tunnel leading to the site of the Duchess of Marlborough's house, which had been demolished in 1785. The tunnel was designed so that servants could reach the house without being seen to cross the lawn. Wimbledon Park House was damaged in the bombing and was demolished in 1959 but the tunnel, 45m (150ft) long, 1.8m (6ft) wide and 2.4 m (8ft) high, still runs under the playing fields of Ricards Lodge School.

The use of underground railway stations as shelters was at first prohibited but it soon became apparent that this rule was impossible to enforce. The nightly trek to these shelters became a matter of course and the 'regulars' would arrive each night with their personal effects and take up their established positions on the platform. Bunk beds made from stretchers were provided in some cases but most people slept on the crowded platforms and, in the case of some disused stations, on the tracks. After months of continual raids this routine became a normal way of life. It was said that a couple, who had met and courted in South Wimbledon underground, married and spent their honeymoon at Colliers Wood underground.

When shelters had to be evacuated, as happened on two occasions at Cottenham Park, the extremes of experience met. The shelterers, shocked by their recent experience of close bombing, found themselves for the first time under an open sky lit by searchlights and gun flashes. The wardens, who were used to this environment, did not at first appreciate how frightened these people were. They could not simply be directed to new places of shelter but had to be formed into small groups and escorted by wardens to alternative public shelters.

Towards the end of the war a new type of indoor shelter made its appearance. This was the Morrison shelter, named after Herbert Morrison, then Minister of Home Security. It consisted of a heavy steel angle frame supporting a sheet of steel plate. Standing only 0.8m (2'.9") high, the top could be used as a table during the day and at night the shelter became a four-poster bed with a strong steel canopy. Steel mesh laid across the base formed a crude form of bedspring and similar mesh around the sides prevented debris falling on to the occupants. These shelters saved many lives, particularly during the flying bomb period when damage to houses was very extensive. However, a warning had to be issued about the use of feather beds or pillows in these shelters. The blast from a nearby bomb could cause bolsters and mattresses to split and the feathers could suffocate those who were sheltering.

Animals were of course frightened by the air raids but many of them seemed to develop a sixth sense. Often a cat or dog would find its way to the air raid shelter minutes before the siren sounded and at the Cottenham Park Ambulance Station the ambulance drivers took advanced warning of bombing from the fact that their pet cat would take shelter underneath a rack of blankets whenever bombs were imminent. Some people were more concerned about their animals than themselves. During the first air raid a milkman who took cover in the public shelter behind the Cottenham Park Ambulance Station, brought his horse with him. There were some 4,000 horses pulling milk floats in the London area and the RSPCA and PDSA tried to care for them and the many thousands of cats and dogs that were rendered homeless. Dogs were less concerned about the loss of their home provided their owner had survived but cats, being territorial, were more difficult to console. There were cases recorded where dogs would dig through the rubble until their paws bled in order to rescue their owners or even a buried cat.

However, the owner of a cat in Griffiths Road that had its tail blown off by a shell simply blamed it for staying out so late. Several other cats are believed to have suffered singed tails from backing into candles in dimly lit shelters and cellars.

Public shelters were built in playing fields and local parks..

TARGET WIMBLEDON

There were a few targets in Wimbledon that were worth deliberate bombing. The railway, being a main line, was obviously important and as a London railway junction it was second only to Clapham Junction. There was also the power station at Durnsford Road and the nearby Southern Railway power station. All these targets were hit but much of the bombing in Wimbledon was of a random nature resulting from poor navigation or the jettisoning of bomb loads. However, there were other targets on the boundaries of Wimbledon that were important to the Germans, such as the KLG Sparking Plug Works on the Portsmouth Road and the numerous factories in the Merton and Morden area. There were also many rumours about the personalities who were living in Wimbledon at the time. Air Chief Marshall Dowding, Chief of Fighter Command, whose residence at 3 St. Mary's Road was commemorated with a blue plaque, and the Rt. Hon. Hore Belisha, then Secretary of State for War, who lived at Warren Farm on Wimbledon Common. The Germans were well aware of this and stated in their propaganda that they would destroy the houses and surrounding area. These threats may have been connected with the raids that occurred in November 1940. The brief respite in the first days of November was a prelude to the heaviest bombing that Wimbledon was to suffer. There were a few bombs on the night of 4th November, two in Arthur Road at the rear of No.24 and 27 and another two in Home Park Road at the rear of No.113. Incendiaries also fell in the Church Road/St. Mary's Road area, where eleven minor fires were started. There were more alerts during the day and night of 5th November but no further incidents. You could not buy fireworks during the war and the traditional displays on this night were now replaced by bursting shells.
On the night of Wednesday 6th November 1940 the Civil Defence Services were stretched to their absolute limit. This was the heaviest raid of the war for Wimbledon. Sixty-seven high explosive bombs fell between 7.35 and 8.35 p.m. The list of incidents for this night covers four closely packed pages.

Reproduced by permission of Mr. Christopher Elliott.

A German Briefing map issued to pilots bombing Wimbledon. The aerial photograph shows Wimbledon Common with the target (in this case the K.L.G. spark plug works on the Portsmouth Road) indicated in heavy outline.

The date at the bottom right hand corner is 1938 and the photograph would have been taken from a civil aircraft before the war.

81

Items 1 to 5 cover the Queens Road area where there were direct hits on No.119 and121 and on No.157 and 159. Other bombs fell on the Council Depot, where a fire was started, and behind No.120 but two bombs falling in the playground of Queens Road School caused the most serious incident. This was now the centre for the rescue and ambulance services and the damage could not have come at a worse time. Four ambulances, a mobile first aid unit and three other vehicles were destroyed. A few hundred yards away in Faraday Road bombs fell at the rear of No.22, 31 and 37 and No.34 and 36 received a direct hit. Another, which fell at the junction of Faraday Road and Evelyn Road, fractured the sewer and burst the gas main. Gas and water mains were also broken in Cromwell Road by a bomb that fell outside No.31. At the control centre, reports came in from all parts of the borough: "No.45 Palmerston Road, serious damage caused by H.E. - No.29, 41 and 56 Princes Road – No.12 The Drive - South Park Gardens – No.7 and 9 St. Mary's Road and Wimbledon High School." At the Queens Road depot, with eight of their vehicles destroyed, rescue teams fought to save the remaining ambulances from the fires that had started and to clear the entrance of rubble so that they could get them onto the road.

In Effra Road two bombs fell on Holy Trinity School, one passing through a first floor classroom and exploding on the ground floor. In the Broadway a bomb landed in front of the Baptist Chapel at the corner of Palmerston Road, blowing away the front of the building. Almost directly opposite, in Stanley Road, one bomb destroyed No.3 and another scored a direct hit on the Seventh Day Adventist Church. A timber yard adjoining the church was soon burning fiercely. In Haydons Road No.226 and 228 were destroyed by a bomb which landed at the rear and No.210 and 212 received a direct hit. A third bomb landed outside No.261 and 263 Haydons Road, one of which was a doctor's surgery. A deep crater was formed and the fronts of the buildings collapsed into the road. In York Road the Sunlight Laundry building was again hit and six bombs fell in the Haydons Road recreation ground. Some of these were within a few yards of the trench shelters but reports show that the morale of the people sheltering in them was excellent and there was no panic.

No.2 Nelson Road was badly damaged by a bomb but another, which landed on the opposite side of the road, failed to explode. In nearby Hardy Road No.2 was wrecked by another bomb from this stick.

A bomb that fell in the front garden of No.4 Cottenham Park Road caused only damage to the roof and windows but Christ Church, the church hall and surrounding houses were damaged. In Copse Hill a bomb fell at the rear of No.7 and another in the front garden of No.28. A third, which landed in the road, caused damage to No.1 and 3 Wool Road. Six more high explosive bombs fell in the grounds of Queen Alexandra's Court but fortunately none of them scored a hit on the buildings.

Miss Rutter, Sister in charge of the All England first aid post, was just leaving her flat in Queen Alexandra's Court when the bombing started and she was hit in the chest by a bomb splinter. She made her way up St. Mary's Road as far as the Vicarage where she took shelter by the garden wall but within a few minutes more bombs fell, one landing in Church Road and another three in the Vicarage garden. Miss Rutter was again injured by a piece of bomb casing but she managed to crawl down Church Road to the first aid post where her injuries were treated by her own staff. On Hill Road two bombs fell simultaneously, one outside No.65 and the other outside No.78 on the opposite side of the road, killing an invalid woman who was in the ground floor room. A No.200 single-decker bus was overturned by the blast and the driver, conductor and passengers were injured and taken to hospital.

All these incidents took place within one hour and reports poured into the control centre at the rate of one every minute. In some cases, where telephone lines were broken, messengers had to be sent to obtain reports on the extent of the incident and the services required. With many of the roads blocked by craters and debris alternative routes had to be found for fire engines and ambulances.

In St. Aubyn's Avenue a bomb that fell at the rear of No.3 and 5 caused only minor damage but in Lake Road, No.6a and 7 Pixham Court were demolished and in Courthope Road there was a direct hit on Belvedere Court, a two storey block of four flats. Nearby at Belvedere Avenue, the back of No.21 was demolished by a bomb that fell in the garden and the rear of No.14 Belvedere Drive was badly damaged. The windows were blown out of all houses in Mansel Road and a number in Raymond Road by two bombs that fell at the rear of No.11 and 13. In St. Mary's Road two bombs fell behind No.7 and 9 and another on the footpath in front. No.9 was very badly damaged and there was roof damage to No.7, 11 and 13. Further along the road the front of No.33 was wrecked but another bomb, which landed in the garden of No.31, failed to explode.

Not all the bombs that fell on the night of 6th November, caused damage to property. A number fell harmlessly on the Common near Westside House and another created a new bunker near the thirteenth green at Wimbledon Park golf course.

It took several days to clear the debris and restore all the services but it is remarkable that in all these incidents no more than four people were killed, seven seriously injured and six slightly injured.

The night of 7th November 1940 brought an incendiary raid at 10.0 pm. Most of the bombs fell on Wimbledon Common between Camp View and the woods by Warren Farm and although there were a number of fires, damage was negligible.

A mixture of high explosives and incendiaries fell on the night of Sunday 10th November between 10.30 and 11.0 p.m. A bomb in Burghley Road damaged only the garage to No.58 but broke a gas main in the road. No.56 Parkside (Heathlands) and Lincoln House, Parkside, each received two H.E. bombs in their gardens. A bomb that fell at the corner of Parkside Gardens and Calonne Road broke only a few windows. There were many incendiary bombs on the Common, on the golf course and on open land at the rear of Hood Road. The last bomb of the night fell at No.6 Queensmere Road where it landed in the piggery.

Only five incendiaries fell in Wimbledon on the night of 11th November but on Tuesday 12th there were several high explosive bombs. The first fell in Avebury Road, between Rayleigh Road and Cliveden Road. A surface water sewer was broken but damage to houses was limited to roofs and glass. The nearby trench shelters in Dundonald Recreation Ground were unharmed. No.11 Rayleigh Road, an unoccupied house, received a direct hit and No.13 was also demolished. Many adjoining houses, including several in Cliveden Road, were badly damaged and two people were killed. A small crater was formed by a bomb at the corner of Oakfield Road and Bathgate Road and the other two bombs that fell that night landed on open ground, one near Windmill Road and the other on Wimbledon Park golf course, about forty yards from Church Road.

No bombs fell in Wimbledon on the following day but damage was caused by two anti-aircraft shells, one hitting Electricity Board transformers in Coppermill Lane and the other at the Ironclad Mantle Factory. The raids on the night of the 15th and 16th November were again heavy. On Friday 15th there were nine incidents involving incendiaries with

84

high explosive attachments. The wardens had become used to dealing with the 1 kg. incendiaries, which had been falling in many hundreds during the previous weeks, but these bombs were now modified to incorporate an explosive booby trap. On the night of the 15th they fell in the Coombe Lane area, between the junction of Copse Hill and the A3. All were effectively dealt with, slight damage being caused to only two houses.

The high explosive bombs fell in the same area. No.6 Lindisfarne Road, near to the Oberon first aid centre, was demolished by a direct hit. Two bombs fell in Melville Avenue, one destroying No.4 and the other causing serious damage to No.6. In Copse Hill a large crater was formed in the road, about fifty yards east of the junction with Almer Road, and at the junction with Coombe Lane two other bombs formed craters and broke a surface water culvert. No.8 Drax Avenue was damaged by a bomb that fell in the garden. Two other bombs fell on Wimbledon Common on either side of Brickfield Cottage, near Stag Ride, and the building was wrecked.

Anti-aircraft shells caused damage to properties at No.13 Springfield Road, 6 and 8 Glendale Drive, where the shell came through a roof and exploded on the ground floor, and at the premises of Lighting Trades Limited in Ravensbury Terrace. A fourth shell that landed in the garden of No.11 Calonne Road, where there was a wardens' post, failed to explode. One other incident appearing in the log book of wardens' post No.14 is worth recording if only for its punctuation: "23.00 hours, message received believed something fell in Alexandra Road about a third of the way up Mr. Wormald, and Mr. Grimshaw sent to investigate."

The night of Saturday 16th November saw another heavy raid on Wimbledon. The alert sounded early that evening at 5.46 pm and the first raid lasted until just before 1.0 am. At 4.35 am the alert sounded again but it was not until 6.00 am on the 17th that the bombs fell. The first two landed in Woodside, one scoring a direct hit on No.55 and the other falling in the road outside No.57, where the gas main and sewer were broken. Queen Alexandra's Court in Lake Road was again damaged, D Block being partly wrecked by a direct hit. Dr. Doody visited the incident and immediately sent for two stretcher parties and three ambulances to back up the rescue team, which had already arrived. Several casualties were trapped under the rubble. Three of these were found to be dead and two others seriously injured and one of whom died on the way to hospital. The other casualties had only minor injuries and were treated at the mobile first aid unit, which arrived shortly afterwards from the Cottenham Park ambulance station.

Houses in Gladstone Road, which had been damaged by previous raids, were hit by the blast from a bomb that fell in the garden of No.83, the home of Alderman Mullins. The rear of houses in Kingswood Road were damaged by a bomb that fell close to the railway line behind No.39 and an anti-aircraft shell exploded in the road outside No.124 Clarence Road. Many bombs fell in Hartfield Road. A bomb landing at the rear of No.69 to 79 caused damage to all these properties. Two others fell in the road, one outside No.79 and the other in front of No.104. Craters were formed in the road and the gas main was fractured. A group of houses was demolished when bombs hit No.116 and 120 and another bomb fell at the rear of Bainshaw's Garage, wrecking the workshops. The Spiritualist Church was badly damaged by a bomb that fell on No.138 Hartfield Road. This was probably a semi-armour-piercing bomb because it penetrated the house and buried itself in the clay subsoil before exploding so that the building was destroyed by the shock wave rather than blast.

No. 38 Gladstone Road, 17th November 1940.

The underground void produced by this type of explosion was known as a camouflet and many years later the cavity was used to form the cellar of the South London Irish Club that now stands on the site.

The worst incident that night was caused by two bombs that fell simultaneously. The first hit the front of a shop, No.58 Hartfield Road, which had been converted into a public air raid shelter, and the second fell in the roadway directly opposite, breaking a large gas main. The shelter normally held sixty-five people but fortunately, on that night, only thirty-nine had taken cover there. Four were killed and another five seriously injured. Three ambulances, three cars and three stretcher parties were soon on the scene and Dr. Cloake arrived shortly after with a mobile first aid unit. Twenty-six had been injured and all were suffering from shock. In the light of the burning gas main, there was some panic but the situation was quickly under control. Those who were not injured were taken to the shelter station at the Central Hall.

Among those killed in this incident were the parents of a young member of the messenger service who was asleep in the basement of the Town Hall only a hundred yards away. He was so exhausted from many nights on duty that his colleagues were unable to wake him to tell him what had happened.

The sirens continued to sound during the next two days but the weather was unsettled and on 18th November there were heavy thunderstorms. The next incidents were on the night of Tuesday 19th November, when bombs fell in South Park Road and Hamilton Road. No.149 and 151 South Park Road were demolished and surrounding buildings damaged. A bomb that fell outside No.62 Hamilton Road burst a gas main and three people were injured.

There were no further incidents recorded until the night of 24th November 1940. At 7.50 pm a bomb fell on No.182 and 184 Florence Road, demolishing these and wrecking No.178 to 188. The houses on the opposite side of the road suffered considerably from the blast and several were badly damaged. A fire broke out among the debris but it was extinguished before it could take hold. A bomb that fell at the junction of South Park Road and Haydons Road, causing a large crater, damaged a number of houses. No.152 to 158 and 187 to 189 Haydons Road were wrecked and there was severe blast damage to shops and to houses in South Park and Cowper Roads. There was similar damage to all houses in North Road caused by a bomb falling at the rear of No.30 to

34 and another that fell on allotments near No.2 East Road damaged adjoining workshops and houses in East Road and South Road. Three people were killed and nineteen injured in this raid.

Although the air raids continued (there were eighty-five alerts during November) incidents were now less frequent and it was not until the night of 3rd December that bombs fell again in the borough. Although only one high explosive bomb fell on this night, and that on the open ground of Wimbledon Park golf course, it was very large and the area of damage was extensive. Blast damage from this one bomb is recorded in Home Park Road, Church Road, St. Mary's Church and Vicarage, Arthur Road, Leopold Road, Wimbledon Hill Road, Somerset Road, Burghley Road and the High Street. A number of incendiaries fell in Copse Hill, near Burdett and Barham Roads but minor damage was caused to only three houses; No.8 Barham Road and No.41 and 89 Copse Hill.

Five days later, on 8th December, another five high explosive bombs fell in Wimbledon and a large number of incendiaries. Two of the bombs fell in Oakfield Road, at the rear of Uplands. Another fell on the centre court of the All England Lawn Tennis Club damaging the stand and part of the roof. A fourth fell in the garden of Orchard Cottage, Queensmere Road and a fifth fell between 23 and 24 Parkside Gardens.

The Centre Court at the All England Lawn Tennis Club, 8th December 1940.

88

A large number of incendiaries fell in two distinct bombing periods. Approximately eighty fires were caused by these but most were efficiently extinguished without delay. Serious fires were started at the rear of Broadway Court, No.78 and 94 The Broadway, 29 Herbert Road, 3 Gap Road, 46 Haydon Park Road and in Kingston Road at No.3 and at the Salvation Army Hall. Appliances had to be called in from other districts to deal with minor fires in Evelyn Road, Queens Road, Craven Gardens, Cromwell Road, Russell Road, Pelham Road and Merton Road. Other incendiaries fell on the Electricity Works, Gap Road Cemetery and at the rear of the Fire Station. Nearly two hundred incendiaries fell on the headquarters of the rescue service at Queens Road School and the drivers had to fight to save their vehicles. Most were saved but several ambulances and other vehicles were damaged. For the rest of December the nights were comparatively quiet. Christmas and Boxing Day 1940 passed without incident but the RAF did not respect the holiday period in their bombing of Germany. Heavy raids on Berlin brought reprisals from the Luftwaffe on the 27th and 29th December. Wimbledon was not seriously affected by either of these raids because the bombing had become more concentrated and more accurate and fewer planes jettisoned their bombs over the suburbs. The bombs that did fall were usually large ones. On the night of 27th December only four bombs fell in the borough and these were all in the Haydon Park Road/Ashcombe Road area. No.102 Haydon Park Road received a direct hit, which destroyed all houses from No. 98 to 106 and badly damaged other houses on each side of the road. A second bomb fell at the rear of No.110 to 112 Haydon Park Road and two bombs fell on the Ark Engraving Company works at Ashcombe Road. Houses in Avondale Road and Cromwell Road were hit by the combined blast from these bombs. On the 29th there were only two incidents in Wimbledon, both caused by anti-aircraft shells. One damaged No.123 Hartfield Road, the other fell down the chimney of No.56 Palmerston Road and exploded in a ground floor room. One man, a soldier home on leave, was seriously injured and a doctor from the mobile first aid unit carried out an operation on the spot. But although he was taken to the nearby Nelson Hospital he subsequently died. No high explosive or incendiary bombs fell in Wimbledon that night but the sky was lit by the fires of London. It was a concentrated raid of high explosives and incendiaries and by morning almost the whole of the square mile of the City of London was burning.

Bomb damage in Haydons Road following the raid of 15th September 1940.

No.85 Home Park Road destroyed on the night of 1st October 1940.

Houses in South Park Road destroyed in a raid on 19th November 1940.

The Seventh Day Adventist Church in Stanley Road, hit by one of sixty-seven high explosive bombs that fell in Wimbledon on the night of 6th November 1940.

THE LAST DAYS OF THE BLITZ

The New Year began quietly. Although the sirens continued to sound the raids were now down to one or two per day and there were no bombing incidents in Wimbledon throughout the month of January 1941. Sometimes a whole day and night would pass without the sirens being sounded. It was not until Monday 17th February that a raid was directed at Wimbledon. At 9.30 that evening a large number of incendiaries fell in the north easterly part of the borough. The majority landed on open ground but many small fires were started in Mount Road, Haslemere Avenue, Dawlish Avenue and Brooklands Avenue and these were dealt with by the fire brigade and wardens. Many more incendiaries fell in Durnsford Road recreation ground.

Another four weeks passed before there was any more activity and then the incidents were caused by anti-aircraft shells that fell in Wycliffe Road and Haydons Road recreation ground. Again a month passed with only occasional raids and no damage in the borough but although most people stayed in their beds at night the blitz was not over and the heaviest raid, as far as London was concerned, had still to come. On the night of the 16th April 1941 a 500 kg. bomb fell in the garden of No.24 Worple Road, near the corner of Francis Grove. It penetrated the ground close to an air raid shelter but failed to explode. Wardens from the nearby post helped to evacuate people from the neighbourhood. At 9.0 pm Mr. Hill, one of these wardens, had come to the end of his tour of duty and returned to his home at 15 Denmark Avenue. At 9.25 pm a Junkers 88 bomber (No.7172 of Kampfgeschwader 76), which was on its way to attack the London docks, was caught momentarily by searchlights. This gave Flt. Lt. Dotteridge and Sgt. Williams in a Beaufighter of No. 219 Squadron the opportunity to attack. The Ju 88 burst into flames and jettisoned its bombs before the crew of four baled out. Three of them, Oberleutenant Moll, Fw. Brahler and Franke survived and were taken prisoner. The aircraft flew on, leaving a trail of burning debris in its path, until it dived into the garden of No.15 Denmark Avenue at 9.34 pm. One engine buried itself in the ground by the kitchen door and the remaining engine and fuselage tore through the adjoining gardens of No.13 and 14 Denmark Avenue. The explosion that followed shook the houses and showered them with fragments and burning petrol. Mr. Hill, who was on the top floor of No.15 and had been about to relax in a warm bath when the plane

93

crashed, used a broom handle to push back pieces of burning wreckage protruding through the bathroom ceiling and then phoned for the fire brigade. They were already on their way but on arrival found that they were faced with the problem of dealing with three fires simultaneously. They were also hampered by the fact that petrol and hydraulic fluid had flowed through to the front gardens and the trees and shrubs were blazing like torches. Eventually the fires were brought under control and damage was restricted to the upper floors of the houses. With the departure of the fire brigade Mr. Hill returned to his bath but was interrupted again when the remains of the bathroom ceiling fell on him.

On that same night, the RAF was carrying out a heavy raid on Berlin and retaliation came two nights later. It was the heaviest raid on London so far but in Wimbledon there were no incidents. Over four hundred bombers took part in a raid that was concentrated on the City. The London landmarks were now familiar to most German pilots and targets were easily identified and bombed. The technique of bombing had also improved. The Germans had formed a Pathfinder Squadron of light bombers, the Kampfgeschwader, or fire raisers, who led the attack with chandelier flares. The main bomber force carried a mixed bomb load of high explosives and incendiary canisters. The H.E.s were used to rip open buildings, which were then set on fire by the incendiaries. Then more H.E.s were dropped to hamper the efforts of the fire and rescue services and finally more incendiaries to stoke the blaze. The glow from the fires that were started on 19th April could be seen every night for almost a week.

On the night of 8th May another aircraft, a Heinkel 111, crashed in Wimbledon. It fell on the first fairway of the Royal Wimbledon golf course and this time the crew did not survive. One made a last minute attempt to bale out but the aircraft was already too low and he was killed as he landed in a garden in Wool Road. The other three members of the crew, Leutenant Stahle, Obergefreiter Weitz and Obergefreiter Senft, were killed in the crash. Wreckage was strewn over a wide area. The plane had been carrying incendiary bombs and as it hit the ground it exploded, shooting balls of blue-white fire into the sky like a giant Roman Candle. In the early hours of the morning an anti-aircraft shell fell outside No. 25 Griffiths Road but damage was limited to broken windows.

An oil filled crater and debris at the rear of No. 13-15 Denmark Avenue where a German bomber crashed on the night of 16th April 1941.

The following day, Saturday 10th May 1941 saw the raid that was to be the end of the blitz and almost the end of London. The raid had not been planned; in fact it was contrary to orders that had recently been issued by Hitler. All available aircraft were required for the surprise attack that the Germans were to launch on Russia on 22nd June and so far as raids on England were concerned the order was to fly limited priority attacks on convoys and industrial targets only. But two nights earlier the RAF had launched massive attacks on Hamburg, Bremen, Emden and Berlin simultaneously. Goaded by this and encouraged by Martin Bormann and his personal pilot Hans Baur, Hitler reached his decision in the early hours of the morning and at 8.0 am on the 10th May orders were issued for a massive raid on London.

The night of 10th May was cold; the coldest May night on record. By midnight the temperature had dropped to below freezing. The moon was full and the sky was cloudless, so that London was laid out as a clear panorama to the five hundred bombers that crossed the coast and followed the Thames up to the London docks. Warehouses were soon blazing but these were not the only targets. Central London and the main railway termini were also marked for destruction. The bombers came in continuous waves throughout the night, returning to their French bases to refuel and rearm. Soon the fires stretched beyond West Ham almost to Romford in the east, to Hammersmith in the west, to the south as far as Norwood and to the north beyond Hampstead. The 1,270 fire appliances of the London County Council were soon fully occupied and another 1,242 were called in from the outer boroughs, including Wimbledon. A further 750 travelled through the night from the Midlands and the West Country. But 3,000 pumps were not enough to cope with the spreading fires. By the early hours of the morning seven hundred acres of London was burning, nearly twice the area damaged by the Great Fire of London in 1666.

Many of the 2,200 individual fires needed thirty pumps or more and the nine conflagrations in the City and at the Elephant and Castle needed at least a hundred pumps each to keep them in check. Even when pumps were available there was often no water to feed them. In the square mile of the City alone, 600,000 gallons of water per minute were required to keep the pumps working. But the water pressure was dropping as one after another of the sixteen and twenty-four inch (0.6m) cast iron water mains, only three feet (1m) below the road surface, were cracked and smashed by high explosive bombs. Altogether six hundred and fifty water mains were broken. In many places the firemen had to stand back and watch as the limp hoses smouldered and fire engines and pumps blistered and then burned. Other pumps were buried under collapsed buildings. The ten million gallons of water stored in emergency tanks was soon exhausted and the Thames was at low ebb. An expanse of black mud separated the firemen from the water. At last four and a half miles (7km) of emergency steel pipeline was laid and the water began to flow again but in many cases it was already too late. Communications broke down as telephone exchanges were destroyed and the roads and bridges were blocked with debris and craters. Six of the City telephone exchanges were out of action. Every bridge over the Thames from Lambeth to the Tower was blocked and eight thousand streets (a third of all in Greater London) were impassable. Seven hundred gas mains were fractured and burning and there was no need for the later waves of bombers to navigate to their target; the flames could be seen as soon as they took off from their airfields a hundred and fifty miles away. Three quarters of all the London docks had been put out of action, as had all the main line railway stations, with the exception of Marylebone, and twenty-nine miles of underground railway had been blocked.

Buckingham Palace, Lambeth Palace, the British Museum, the Tower of London and Westminster Abbey were all burning and the Chamber of the House of Commons, the Temple Church and seven Wren churches, including St. Clement Dane's and St. Stephen's, Walbrook, were gutted. St. Paul's was saved only by the most strenuous efforts to keep the surrounding fires at bay. St. Thomas and the Greycoat Hospitals had been badly damaged and the Queen's Hall destroyed. Several hundred factories and warehouses, including seventy-one key factories producing aircraft parts and instruments, had been demolished. At 1.0 am emergency working had been introduced. Fires had to be treated on a strict priority basis. No attempt could be made to deal with fires among the eleven thousand houses that had been destroyed, and warehouses full of shoes, candles, brandy, flour and jam were left to burn themselves out. The twenty-three acres of vaulted warehousing under Waterloo station burned for four days. By the time the last bomb fell at 5.37 am on New Scotland Yard, firemen and rescue workers were exhausted to the point of collapse. Mr. Gates, who led a rescue team from Wimbledon, recalled how men lay down in gutters still running with water from the hoses and fell asleep.

Wimbledon escaped lightly with only four people killed and six injured, compared with the fourteen hundred killed and eighteen hundred seriously injured in London that night. A bomb that fell in Hartfield Crescent demolished No.87 to 91 and wrecked railway carriages in the nearby sidings. In Burghley Road, bombs fell at the rear of No.2 and 8 and at the junction with Marryat Road. Large craters were formed but damage was slight. Two more bombs fell in the car park of the All England Lawn Tennis Club close to Dairy Walk and another in Oakfield Road, breaking a gas main and damaging several houses. The Gap Road/Plough Lane area was again saturated with incendiaries but there were no serious fires, which was fortunate in view of the depleted strength of the fire service.

The following morning few people in Wimbledon realised how serious the London raid had been. There were no trains running into London and power and gas services were interrupted but otherwise the only clues to the extent of the damage were the glows from the fires that continued to burn for eleven days and nights and the flakes of charred paper that fell from the sky — the remains of 250,000 books that had been burned at the British Museum.

The raid on 10th May marked the end of the blitz. It would have been easy for the German Air Force to follow up the devastation with further raids. They had lost only fourteen aircraft. Official but secret estimates in this country were that one, or at the most two, more raids of this magnitude would be sufficient to destroy the whole of London. At the main conflagrations the firemen had felt themselves being sucked towards the fires by the tremendous convection currents. If these fires had linked together the result would have been a fire-storm, with hurricane force winds roaring through the city, as happened in Dresden. Fortunately for London the Germans were already committed to the invasion of Russia on 22nd June and by the time they realised how near their attack had been to total success, the bulk of the Luftwaffe was already on its way to the East.

THE DRAB YEARS

The air raids were now infrequent. There were occasional warnings and some minor activity but apart from a few anti-aircraft shells no incidents were reported in Wimbledon between May 1941 and February 1944. Attitudes had hardened and life had become grim. Now that the nightly air raids had finished there was time to brood and to grumble. In the interminable queues for food the talk was of the smallness of rations and the high prices. Clothing was strictly rationed. Some wealthier people would pass on clothes and shoes to those less well off in exchange for clothing coupons so that they could update their wardrobes or replace children's outgrown clothes and shoes.

The streets themselves were shabby. It was not possible to walk any distance without being reminded of the war by the piles of yellow rubble smelling of damp plaster, coal gas and clay. Most of the shop windows in Wimbledon Broadway had been blown out and had been replaced by plywood or boarding, with small glazed apertures for the display of goods. The exhilaration of the early days of bombing had gone. There was no more dancing in the streets at the news of how many German aircraft had been shot down. Even the slogans on the posters had changed: "Go to It" had been replaced by "Britain can Take It."

At first some people found it difficult to sleep at night without the background noise of gunfire. Although there was no activity there were constant reminders of the raids. The blackout was still rigidly enforced and on nights when there was no moon the darkness would be so complete that it would not be possible to walk anywhere without a torch to pick out the pavements, kerbs and street furniture. However, so many people were now using torches that batteries were in short supply. The No.8 battery used in most pocket torches practically disappeared. The only advantage of the blackout was that on clear nights you could see literally millions of stars.

Identity cards and gas masks still had to be carried at all times. Many people had replaced the original cardboard boxes in which the gas masks had been issued with more fashionable containers or had covered them with leather-cloth. The tops of pillar-boxes were coloured lime green with a paint that was sensitive to mustard gas. Silver barrage balloons still hung like bloated fish in the sky.

Some local landmarks had been altered so that they would be less recognisable from the air. The windmill on Wimbledon Common had one of its sails removed and this was only replaced when the sails were renewed in 1959. Less fortunate was Wimbledon Theatre, which had only been built thirty years before the war. The features above the dome, namely the 'temple', the illuminated globe and the gilt 'angel', were all removed and it would take fifty years of campaigning to get them replaced.

Another local feature that had disappeared, but for rather different reasons, was the stone sculpture of a stag that had stood on the roof of Stag Lodge, adjoining St. Mary's Church. This heraldic beast had been there since the house was built as the entrance lodge to Earl Spencer's Wimbledon Park estate and the owners were concerned that it might be damaged if any bombs fell nearby. So they called in a builder and asked him to remove it – which he did, using a sledge- hammer!

The character of many ordinary roads had been changed by the removal of iron railings from parks and the front gardens of the Victorian houses. It was said that they were required for munitions but the main purpose was to bring home the need for a continued war effort. In fact the cast iron from which most of them were made was of little use and thousands of tons of them were dumped in the North Sea. In its small way the removal of these railings probably caused more lasting damage to the character of this and other London suburbs than the bombing.

Roads were often deserted. Although public transport continued to function, private cars, other than those required for civil defence or business purposes, could not be used. Petrol was strictly rationed for official business and every journey had to be accounted for and recorded. The headlamps of vehicles were masked leaving only narrow slits through which a gleam of light shone on the road and traffic lights were blacked out except for a small cross in the centre of each light. Whenever a car was parked it had to be immobilized by removing a vital part such as the rotor arm from the distributor.

Bicycles came into their own but spares and replacements were difficult to find and tyres were patched and patched again. The windows of buses, trams and trains were covered with coarse netting fixed with a strong adhesive to prevent glass from splintering if it were broken by blast. A small clear diamond shape was left in the centre of

Petrol pumps were protected by surrounding them with sandbags.

each window so that passengers could check their progress. Some rail passengers would pick away at the edge of the netting to increase the size of the opening and this led to posters being produced in which a friendly ticket inspector was shown saying: "I trust you'll pardon my correction, that stuff is there for your protection". Passengers retaliated by adding: "I thank you for that information but I cannot see the bloody station".

Not that seeing the station was of any great assistance because station names, along with signposts and street names had been removed or painted out in the early days when invasion was thought to be imminent. Train journeys at night were particularly difficult and were often accomplished by counting the number of stations. Blinds had to be drawn to obscure the dim blue lights that illuminated each compartment and stepping out of a train at an unlit station was a hazardous operation when there was a chance of getting out on the wrong side and landing on the track instead of the platform. Nor was there any encouragement to travel at all, with notices at stations asking: "Is Your Journey Really Necessary?"

101

Entertainment for many people consisted of a weekly visit to the cinema, as much to see the newsreel as the main feature. There were often long queues and people were only admitted in ones and twos as other people came out. This meant that you often went in half way through a film. Some people saw this as an advantage when you were watching a "Who done it" film, because you not only did not know 'who done it', you didn't know who they had done. Listening to the 9 o'clock news was a ritual that was religiously observed and the sound of Big Ben, which preceded it, gave a sense of permanence and reassurance that was much needed. There were no weather forecasts for security reasons. In a lighter vein, and with an equally devoted following, was the weekly broadcast of Tommy Handley in ITMA. Some people listened to the German propaganda broadcasts of 'Lord Haw-Haw' and found them equally amusing. Early morning programmes were devoted to recipes designed to eke out the meagre rations. Fish, one of the few unrationed foods, featured prominently in these. Almost all foods were rationed. Cakes were still available but seemed to be made from sawdust. One type of cake was known as a 'Nothing cake' because apart from flour and dried egg it contained none of the usual ingredients.

Rationing had not begun until January 1940 and then only for bacon, ham, sugar and butter. General meat rationing began in March and was based upon value so that it was possible to obtain a larger quantity by choosing the cheaper cuts rather than prime cuts. The weekly ration was 1s.10d. for adults (later reduced to 1s.1d.) and 11d for children under six. Stews made the meat ration go further but there were no onions to be found following the fall of France and the Channel Islands. By July, tea (2oz. per week) and margarine (4oz,) had joined the list. In 1941 jam, marmalade and syrup were rationed followed by cheese (1oz. per week). Eventually the points system was introduced for all canned goods, condensed milk, breakfast cereals and biscuits. The control of stocks then became much easier for the government because when products were in short supply the number of points required to buy them could be increased and when there was a surplus they could be reduced. Sausages, made largely from bread and offal, were unrationed. As soon as it was known that a butcher had some sausages in stock a long queue would form outside. In fact there were queues for most things and people would often join them not knowing what they were for but on the basis that whatever it was must be worth having.

There were two Government sponsored British Restaurants in the Wimbledon area. They served a very basic menu that included such 'delicacies' as whale meat, snoek and 'Woolton Pie'. The pie, named after the Minister of Food, contained carrots, parsnips, turnips and potatoes. It was not very popular. Children under five, who were holders of green coloured ration books, were entitled to fresh fruit when it was available but even they did not see a banana until the end of the war.

The keeping of chickens and even pigs was encouraged. Pig clubs were set up on wasteland with residents having shares in the pigs and supplying their vegetable peelings and scraps for the food. There was a black market in some foods but it was not as extensive as generally supposed. There was a story that the purchaser of some black market tinned food complained that it had 'gone off' and was told: "This is not for eating, it is for buying and selling".

Books were in short supply and were printed on poor quality paper. Although hardback books still had dust jackets these were usually reused and if you took them off you would find the title of another book on the reverse side. However, an appeal in Wimbledon for old books, to help restock damaged libraries and to send to the troops, produced over 100,000 volumes. There were few toys for children and those that were available were often crudely made as the toy factories had been turned over to war production. The Lines Brothers' factory, previously devoted to manufacturing Triang toys, produced over one and a half million Sten guns, magazines for Bren guns and the ammunition feed mechanisms for Spitfires and Hurricanes. Many of these were tested on the premises and the sound of machine gun fire could often be heard in South Wimbledon.

Although the bombing had ended, the civil defence services had to stay on the alert and all posts had to be manned. However, after many months of inactivity morale had sunk to such a low pitch that the chief warden said that he had thoughts of asking the RAF to drop a few bombs on the Common so as to keep everyone on their toes! The common itself had changed. Trenches had been dug at all strategic points and concrete dragons' teeth acted as barriers to tanks. Rows of posts had been erected across open spaces to prevent aircraft or gliders from landing and the area between West Place and Parkside was covered with allotments. A large ammunition dump was hidden in the trees on the eastern bank of Queensmere and barbed wire marked the boundaries of the army camp near the Windmill. The gravel pits and dunes, that were then a feature of the common, were marked with the tracks of the Bren gun carriers that practised there. These gravel pits were later filled with the rubble from the bombed houses of Wimbledon. Beside Rushmere stood an army assault course and a Bailey bridge was erected across the pond.

Parts of the Common that were not used for any of these activities were turned over to growing wheat and for a time a small camp near the end of Lauriston Road housed prisoners of war who tended the crops. 'Dig for Victory' was the call of the day and private gardens were dug up and planted with vegetables (one local patriot dug up his lawn and planted asparagus). In the Wimbledon Borough News there was a letter complaining that South Park Gardens still had grass and flowerbeds when it should have been ploughed up.

The wardens, bored by inactivity, returned to light spotting. Every week the Borough News listed people who had been fined for infringing the blackout regulations. A minor sensation was caused at one post when news was received of signals being flashed from a house in Arthur Road but the flashing lights were eventually tracked to some fragments of mirror that had been hung over a seed bed and were reflecting the moonlight. The various Civil Defence services organised shows and entertainments for the children who were now beginning to return from evacuation and efforts were made to brighten the drabness of life by turning the results of disaster to advantage. Bombsites were soon taken over by the children as adventure playgrounds. A game played on one site in Faraday Road involved holding a lighted candle under the percussion cap of a 20mm cannon shell.

The boarding on shop windows became the background for bright posters. The post office and newsagents in Arthur Road showed posters for the magazines John Bull and Illustrated, but the owner refused to display one that read, 'Get your Woman here'.

HIT AND RUN

The raid that occurred on 4th February 1944 came as a shock. It had been so long since there had been any serious air raids that everyone was taken by surprise. Only five bombs fell and one of those, which landed at the rear of All Saints Church, failed to explode. But they were large bombs and damage was widespread with twenty-seven houses being destroyed, forty-eight seriously damaged and a further three hundred and twenty suffering minor damage. No.24 to 28 Deburgh Road were destroyed and the Sultan Public House and houses in Norman Road were also badly damaged. A number of houses were affected by a bomb that fell at the rear of No.93 and 95 Victory Road and in Quicks Road No.69 to 72 were demolished. One of those killed in Deburgh Road was a seventy-four year old woman who was only visiting for the night. Five other people died and twenty-five were injured but there were some remarkable escapes. One bomb completely destroyed an Anderson shelter but the family, including two children, had stayed in bed and were quite safe. Another man, also in bed, found himself revealed to the public gaze as the complete front of his house was blown out. Some Canadian soldiers who were passing helped to rescue him. A dog, which had been buried in the ruins of a house, was found because its tail was sticking out from the debris. As soon as the rescuers started to dig the tail began to wag and the dog was rescued unharmed. A cat that was also buried managed to dig itself out after four days.

This was the first of the hit and run raids. They generally involved only one or two aircraft that flew over, dropped their bombs and fled for the coast. On 13th February there was a short raid during which no bombs fell on Wimbledon but the Regal cinema in The Broadway was damaged by an anti-aircraft shell. A few days later, on 19th February, several large bombs fell in the Wimbledon area. The first, shortly before 1.0 am, landed outside Verran's Garage in Merton Road. The explosion tore up the tramlines and damaged all main services. A large gas main was broken and burned fiercely for some time and the garage and petrol filling station adjoining was burnt out. On the opposite side of Merton Road two large houses, No.169 and 171, were demolished and the Labour Exchange, which was a temporary building, was gutted by fire.

No.169-171 Merton Road, destroyed on the night of 19th February 1944.

Many surrounding houses were severely damaged and the blast affected houses in Hamilton Road, Quicks Road, Cecil Road, Balfour Road, Merton High Street, Pelham Road, Griffiths Road and The Broadway. Eighty-three people were injured in this incident.

On the edge of the Common, at the junction of Clifton Road and Southside, a bomb that fell on the grass verge demolished Oakholme (No. 11 Southside) a large eighteenth century house. The house was not occupied at the time but the gardener, who lived in a cottage adjoining, was killed. Clifton House (No.10) and Rushmere (No.12) were badly damaged and The Priory, King's College School and No.8 and 9 Southside were also hit by the blast. Four people in these adjoining houses were injured. Another bomb fell on The Cottage (No.82 Ridgway), which stood at the rear of King's College School, close to Wright's Alley. This house was completely destroyed and adjoining houses in the Ridgway lost their windows and roofs.

A third bomb scored a direct hit on No.5 The Downs and No.6 and 8 were very badly damaged. No.5 and 6 were Catholic homes of rest for the elderly. There was not a single wall of No.5 left standing and rescue workers had to clear vast piles of debris to reach the people buried

106

beneath it. All available rescue teams were called in and they worked in four-hour shifts throughout the night. It was very cold with snow drifting down but in the first twelve hours they managed to move between sixty and eighty tonnes of rubble. The morale of those who were rescued was very high. The main concern of one elderly resident who was trapped in the basement where gas was leaking was that he was not allowed to smoke a cigarette. Another couple were found to have tied their arms together so they should not be separated. More ambulances arrived from the Richmond area and in the early hours of the morning the rescue workers were stunned to see a group of nuns from St. Teresa's hospital, further along the road, arriving to help. What made the sight particularly memorable was that each nun had the hem of her habit tucked into heavy rubber boots and was wearing a steel helmet. The following day rescue teams from Mitcham were called in to help. Five of the residents had been killed and another twenty-two injured. Ambulances stood by to take them to hospital as they were brought out of the wreckage. Local Girl Guides helped to salvage wheelchairs and personal belongings.

The combined effect of these three bombs caused damage to buildings as far away as The Crooked Billet, Westside and the whole length of the Ridgway. One other bomb fell that night, on the east goods railway yard, near Alexandra Road, causing damage to the railway tracks. In the Queensmere Road/Parkside area, a number of incendiaries fell, resulting in fires at No.6 Queensmere Road, where serious damage was caused, and at Homestead, Haven Cottage, Heathlands and Castle Towers on Parkside. Other incendiaries fell in the Merton Hall Road area, starting fires at No.69 and 83, and the nurses' quarters on the top floor of the Nelson Hospital were set on fire. Many patients had to be evacuated from the building, including some who had only just been brought in from the other bombing incidents. Wardens helped nurses and stretcher-bearers to carry out the evacuation.

An elderly woman who had been slightly injured in one of the bombing incidents was being carried on a stretcher and was concerned that the warden might drop her. The warden told her that she was "As safe as houses", which was a rather tactless phrase to use to someone who had just lost her home, especially as he then slipped on the polished floor and fell with the stretcher on top of him.

The following night bombs fell in front of Clock House and Heathfield House in Windmill Road, both of which were seriously damaged. A bomb that fell at the rear of Oakfield in Somerset Road caused blast damage only and two others that fell on Wimbledon Park golf course, one near Church Road and the other near Home Park Road, broke windows and roof tiles on adjoining houses, the All England Lawn Tennis Courts and the Club House. A fifth bomb landed at the rear of No.95 Home Park Road, destroying the back of the house and damaging No.93 and 97. The blast damage was extensive and windows were blown out as far as No.63 Home Park Road. Two anti-aircraft shells fell harmlessly on Wimbledon Park golf course.

In the early hours of 23rd February a large number of incendiaries fell in the Haydons Road area. About half of these failed to ignite and the majority fell in open spaces but about thirty fires were started in Haydons Road, Gap Road, Durnsford Road, Plough Lane and Avondale Road. The fire service attended sixteen of these, which threatened to get out of control, including their own fire station at St. Peter's Hall. At 10.40 the same night more high explosive bombs fell in the Wimbledon area. A bomb demolished No.26 and 28 Fairlawn Road and killed two people. At Kingswood Road No.45 was severely damaged by a second bomb. The other bombs that fell that night all failed to explode. Wardens set out to search for them but they were quite difficult to find. One at No.3 Sherwood Road had fallen very close to the house between the front door and the adjoining bay window. Another fell between No.5 and 6. A third penetrated the roof, first floor and a grand piano before coming to rest on the ground floor of a house in Sherwood Road.

In Fairlawn Road a bomb fell close to the side entrance of No.25, leaving a hole immediately outside the kitchen door, and another fell in the garden of No.119 Graham Road, near the railway. At Durnsford Road a bomb that failed to explode landed a few feet from the rear of No.228 and in Wellington Road one penetrated the roof of a shed near the entrance gates to the Neuchatel Works. Many people had to be evacuated from these areas until the bombs had been cleared. A number of incendiaries fell on Wimbledon Stadium starting a serious fire. The unoccupied club premises, comprising offices, stores, part of the grandstand and kennels were burnt out. Two of the firemen fighting the blaze were seriously injured. An anti-aircraft shell landed near the school in Russell Road that had been hit by previous bombing.

108

The following night there was another raid in which the anti-aircraft fire was particularly heavy. Shortly before 10.0 pm an anti-aircraft shell exploded in the forecourt of Wimbledon station, on the Hill Road side. A number of shops were damaged, including Lavells, Rickett Smiths, W.H. Smith and the Electricity showrooms and nine people were injured. One, a Canadian soldier, died shortly after admission to hospital. A few incendiaries fell in the area of Lucien Road, but wardens and firewatchers put these out before any damage could be caused. The all-clear sounded before midnight but a few minutes later another raid started. A high explosive bomb fell in the garden of Ormindale (37 Burghley Road) causing a large crater in the garden extending into the road. Mains and services were broken but only a few tiles were disturbed on Ormindale itself. A number of explosive incendiary bombs fell on the Wimbledon Common golf course and the Drax Estate, starting fires at No.1a Dunstall Road and 6 Ernle Road. No.33 Faraday Road was badly damaged by a shell and another fell at No.121 Dora Road.

Five bombs fell on the golf course on Wimbledon Common but failed to explode. Shortly after midnight Mr. Ball, the Chief Warden, was called out to investigate a suspected unexploded bomb that had fallen in the army camp site near the Windmill. He found a crater approximately six feet deep and fifteen feet diameter (2m x 4.5m), and, from scraps of evidence found in the crater, he was able to establish that it was an unexploded 1,000 kg. bomb. Mr. Ball decided that it was unlikely to go off as it was not usual to fit delayed action fuses to this type of bomb. However, bombs of this particular size were normally dropped in pairs and if a second one had fallen elsewhere on the Common and failed to explode it could involve a very difficult search among the bracken and undergrowth in order to recover it. Next morning in daylight, a second crater was found on the perimeter of the camp and Mr. Ball returned to investigate. He was searching the crater for evidence that this was the twin of the one that had been identified the night before, when a sergeant major from the camp appeared at the edge of the crater with a young ATS girl who asked if the bombs were very large. The sergeant major said that he thought they could only have been about 'fifty-pounders' judging by the size of the crater. Turning to Mr. Ball, who was in the crater, he asked: "What do you think down there?" Mr. Ball looked up and replied that in fact the bomb weighed over a tonne and

109

hadn't gone off yet. There was a stunned silence before the sergeant major and the ATS girl disappeared over the horizon.

Although it was not known at the time, the raid of 24th February 1944 was to be the last conventional air raid on Wimbledon. The next air raid report, on Friday 16th June, shows one incident only when a pilotless aircraft fell at 3.30 am at Cliveden Road. This was the first of the V weapons, the flying bomb.

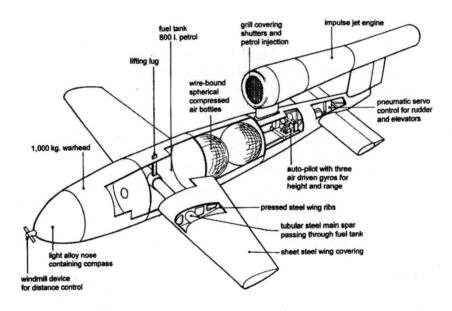

The construction of a flying bomb

THE FLYING BOMBS

In June 1944 when the first flying bombs arrived many people, who did not understand the true nature of these weapons, greeted them with jubilation. The newspapers were full of the D-Day landings and morale had been given a tremendous boost. The sight of enemy aircraft apparently crashing in flames was greeted with cheers. But for those in Civil Defence, who had been forewarned that a secret weapon was on the way, this was no time for celebration. When the wardens inspected the extent of damage at the Cliveden Road incident they were filled with despair. Seventeen houses, No 39 to 51 and 36 to 54 were completely destroyed and No.53, 55 and 56 were damaged beyond repair. All the remaining houses in Cliveden Road had suffered damage as well as houses in Rayleigh Road and Wilton Cresent. Damage to roofs and windows was spread over a wide area, including property in Merton, and twelve people had been killed and fifty-three injured.

The weapon was known by a number of names. Its correct title, according to German sources, was Vergeltung 1, or revenge weapon No.1, abbreviated to V-1. The first incident reports refer to the weapon as a robot plane or pilotless aircraft but in later reports the term flying bomb or fly-bomb was used. The general public soon found their own names for these weapons, the most popular being buzz bombs and doodle bugs.

The flying bomb had a steel torpedo shaped body with short stubby wings and a high mounted engine on the tail. At the front of the body was a warhead of 1,000 kg. of high explosive and behind this were two pressurized spheres containing fuel for the engine. The weapon was driven by a simple form of jet engine, known as a pulse-jet. This comprised a combustion chamber with a spring-loaded valve at the front and an open exhaust at the rear. The valve was made from a series of flaps or louvres that opened to allow air to be forced into the chamber as the weapon moved forward. Fuel was then injected and ignited in the combustion chamber and the resultant explosion forced the louvres at the front to close and the gasses to be ejected at the rear. The sound produced by this engine was a deep-throated rumble, more like a large motorcycle engine than a conventional aircraft engine. In the tail of the weapon was the guidance equipment, which included a gyrocompass and a timing device that sent the bomb into its final dive. It was generally supposed at the time that the bomb's engine stopped when it had run out of fuel but in fact a pre-set mechanism released two bolts at the rear of the body that locked the control surfaces and sent the aircraft into a steep dive. It was this steep dive that threw the remaining fuel to the front of the fuel tanks and stalled the engine. However, the technical details did not interest those who dived for cover and counted the seconds between the time that the engine stopped and the bomb finally burst.

Normally the V-1 went into a tight spin and dived onto its target almost vertically but on some occasions the speed built up by its steep dive would cause it to pull out and continue its flight for a considerable distance. Thousands were shot down as they crossed the coast and many others were intercepted by fighters or gunfire before they reached the London area. However, although their course was predictable and the V-1s could not take evasive action like a conventional aircraft, they were not an easy prey for fighters. Firstly they were very fast and our fighters had difficulty keeping up with them. Secondly if you fired your guns from the traditional distance of 100-200m and a bullet hit the 1,000 kg. warhead you could be engulfed in the resulting explosion. A technique developed by some fighter pilots was to fly alongside a V-1 so closely that the wing of the fighter could be used to flick the flying bomb over onto its back. This upset its guidance system and made it crash out of control.

On the night of 17th June another flying bomb landed on open ground owned by the council near Beverley meads. No crater was formed as these weapons exploded on impact and the thin casing to the warhead meant that it could not penetrate into the ground. Blast damage, however, was extensive as is shown by the fact that in some cases as many as three or four hundred houses were damaged by the blast from one bomb. Three more flying bombs fell on 19th June, the first at 3.40 am on Wimbledon Park golf course, causing blast damage to houses in Home Park Road, Arthur Road, Church Road and St. Mary's Road. There were no casualties. At 6.30 in the morning another landed on Wimbledon Hill, hitting the footpath outside Emerson Court flats. The whole front of the building was blown out and properties adjoining and on the other side of the road were seriously damaged. Three people were killed, including two police inspectors who were in a car on Wimbledon Hill, and sixteen others were injured. Blast damage from this bomb affected properties in The Grange, Ridgway Place, St. George's Road, Alexandra Road, Park Road, Woodside, St. Mary's Road, Church Road and the High Street. The third flying bomb fell at 8.35 am on Dennis Park Crescent, near the corner of Burstow Road. All the houses at the junction of these two roads were demolished and there was extensive damage to houses in the Lower Downs housing estate. Twenty-four people were injured. Although there were only three bombs involved in this raid, as compared to the multiple incidents in a conventional bombing raid, the damage was so widespread that it was necessary to call in additional wardens from outside the London area. Teams of wardens were brought in from Salisbury, Market Harborough and Newark and they were billeted in local schools and halls.

After the Blitz many evacuees had returned to Wimbledon but now a new evacuation was organized on a massive scale. At 3.0pm.on the afternoon of 20th June a flying bomb fell in the garden at the rear of 33 Holland Avenue. No.11 to 41 Holland Avenue and 170 to 176 Copse Hill were destroyed or seriously damaged and damage was caused to all houses between Lindisfarne Road and Coombe Lane as well as to houses in Beverley Avenue, Hood Road, Preston Road, Barham Road, Burdett Avenue, Melville Avenue and Coombe Lane. Fifteen people were injured. In the early hours of the following morning two more flying bombs fell, one on the John Barker sports ground in Church Road, causing damage to the pavilion and blast damage to surrounding houses, and another at 4.15 a.m. on the south side of Rushmere pond, Wimbledon Common. This caused damage to No.1 and 6 Southside and to all houses on The Green. Minor damage was caused to houses in Lauriston Road, in the Ridgway from the Swan Hotel to Lingfield Road, the High Street, Parkside and Parkside Avenue. A few hours later a flying bomb was brought down by anti-aircraft fire. It landed on Wimbledon Park golf course, wrecking the clubhouse and damaging a number of houses in the area. At about the same time a bomb fell on the Wandle Valley Sewage Works, breaking glass and damaging the roofs of houses nearby.

At 2.04 am on Monday 23rd June, a flying bomb hit the rear of No.33 Faraday Road. Many houses in this area had been damaged by previous bombing and incendiaries and in this incident No.23 to 37 were completely destroyed and all houses from 21 to 67 badly damaged. Fronts of houses on the opposite side of the road were hit by the blast and the new extension to Effra Road School was destroyed. Houses on both sides of Effra Road, from Trinity Road to Evelyn Road, were damaged to varying degrees. In this incident one person was killed, seven others taken to hospital and a further twenty-five treated for minor injuries. During the night another flying bomb was shot down by fighter aircraft. This one crashed on Wimbledon Common in the vicinity of Warren Farm and Robin Hood Road.

No other bombs fell on Wimbledon until 29th June, although many were heard to pass overhead. They flew along regular routes and the areas over which they passed came to be known as 'doodlebug alley'. At 10.35 in the morning of the 29th a V-l landed on the Southern Railway near the washing shed by Gap Road Bridge. It is believed to have flown along the length of the railway line and between the supports of Gap Road Bridge before hitting a train that was entering the washing shed. The driver of the train was killed and damage was caused to the railway flyover and adjoining buildings. No.25 to 28 Landgrove Road were destroyed and many other houses severely damaged, including houses in Waldemar Road, Strathearn Road, Kenilworth Avenue, Gap Road, Pitt Crescent and Ashcome Road. Damage was also caused in Kingston Road and Merton High Street, from Cecil Road to Grove Road, by a bomb that fell in Nelson Gardens.

At 8.55 that evening St. Matthew's Church in Spencer Road was destroyed, together with houses No.2 to18, and fire broke out among the wreckage. Many houses in Spencer Road, Durham Road, Richmond Road and Amity Grove also suffered damage. There were eighteen casualties including one fatality in the first incident and forty casualties in the Spencer Road incident. Many people were rendered homeless and had to find shelter at the Southfields Central Hall and the Village Hall in Lingfield Road. The WVS set up enquiry points and blitz information bureaux in Kenilworth Avenue and Durham Close.

At 10.35am. on Friday 30th June, No.133 to 143 and 98 to 102 Cambridge Road were destroyed by another flying bomb. Many houses were damaged in Cambridge Road, Richmond Road, Oakwood Road, Laurel Road and Coombe Lane. Three people were killed, twenty-five injured and many others sent to rest centres. In the afternoon a flying bomb was shot down on the Royal Wimbledon golf course by an RAF plane; it landed on the fifth fairway and Warren Farm suffered damage from the blast. In the evening, houses in Queensmere Road and Parkside were hit by the blast from a bomb that fell in the Wandsworth area.

Reports of where the V-1s fell in Central and South London were suppressed as far as possible but the Government leaked details of incidents in North London in the hope that the Germans would be fooled into thinking that they were overshooting their main target. They might then shorten the range of their flying bombs so that more would fall in open country to the south of London. Similarly when the V-2 rockets started to arrive only those that fell in the south were reported in the hope of transferring the majority to the north of London. It is doubtful that these policies worked because the Germans were able to obtain quite a good idea of where their weapons were landing by reading the obituaries in The Times and The Daily Telegraph. However, it is true that although Wimbledon received many V-1s, not a single V-2 fell in the borough.

At 2.50 the following morning another flying bomb, outside No.10 to 14 Melbury Gardens, formed a shallow crater in the footpath and part of the roadway. The gas main was broken and burst into flames, destroying a number of army lorries that were parked in this road. No.3 to 19 and 10 to 14 Melbury Gardens were demolished. Further damage was caused to houses in Durham Road, Cottenham Park Road, Panmuir Road and Cambridge Road, many of the buildings having been damaged by the previous incidents but only three people were injured in this raid.

On Tuesday 4th July 1944 the railway line was again hit by a flying bomb which fell at 10.02 am, just east of Durnsford Road Bridge. Elm Lodge and Wellington House in Durnsford Road, were badly damaged. Six people were injured and damage was caused to houses in Arthur Road, The Crescent, Crescent Gardens and Strathmore Road.

Two bombs fell on 5th July. The first, shortly after mid-day, landed on the King's College School playing fields, damaging the swimming pool and the main building. School Certificate examinations were in progress at the time and so that the bombing should not interrupt these they were carried out in the shelters. This meant that the rest of the school had to stay in the classrooms and boys and staff had to dive under desks to avoid the flying glass when the bomb exploded.

Nearby houses in Lansdowne Road and the Ridgway were badly damaged. Wimbledon College suffered only slightly from the blast and, because there was not adequate shelter, the examination candidates at this school had been sent away to a Jesuit boarding school in Derbyshire. Roofs and windows were damaged, as far away as Arterberry Road and The Crooked Billet and there was minor damage in most of the roads leading off the Ridgway. In the houses nearest the explosion there were six casualties. At 5.41 the same afternoon a flying bomb landed on Wimbledon Common, opposite Calonne Road, causing widespread but minor damage.

Two days later in the early hours of 7th July, a flying bomb hit houses in Herbert Road, demolishing No.29 to 51 and 22 to 38. St. Andrew's Hall was destroyed and St. Andrew's Church was badly damaged. Many other houses were partly wrecked, including Herbert Villas and houses in Graham Road. In Hartfield Road the blast hit Bainshaw's Garage, which had been damaged in an earlier raid, and No.81 to 89. There was minor damage to properties over a very wide area, including Dundonald Road, Kingswood Road, Wilton Crescent, Mayfield Road and Gladstone Road. Twelve people were taken to hospital and another sixteen were treated for minor injuries. The WVS at the Village Hall in Lingfield Road had to deal with one hundred and fifteen people who had been rendered homeless and fifty of these were subsequently transferred to Southfields Central Hall.

At seven minutes past nine on the morning of 10th July the air raid warning sounded again and before the sirens had died away a flying bomb had crashed at the rear of No.17 Southey Road, close to Pelham Road School. Normally there would have been several hundred children in the school playground but due to the difficulties of travel and the frequency of warnings, the school day did not always start punctually. On this morning there were only twenty-eight children and they had all taken shelter within the school before the bomb landed. Pelham Road School had no shelters but the whole of the ground floor had been barricaded with sandbags, filled and stacked by parents during the early days of the war. None of the children was injured but in the adjoining houses there were many casualties. One person was killed and ninety-two people were injured, fifty-three of these being sent to hospital. Cross Road was obliterated, No.9 to 17 Southey Road demolished and No.3 to 7 wrecked beyond recognition. On the other side of the road No.12 to 14 were badly damaged and in Palmerston Road No.1 to 11 were destroyed or wrecked. Minor damage extended from Kingston Road to The Broadway and from Gladstone Road to the far end of Pelham Road. A piece of the bomb fell at the feet of a boy in Southey Road who picked it up as a souvenir and then dropped it because it was still hot from the explosion. That piece is now in the Wimbledon Society's Museum. The Incident Officer called out Sappers who were training at the nearby Technical College to assist in clearing the debris. Sounds of crying led rescuers to a baby trapped under the rubble.

Damage was caused in the Wandle Road/Leyton Road area by a bomb which fell on the Merton Board Mills on 12th July and in the morning of the 14th July, just before 10.0 am, a flying bomb demolished houses in Plough Lane and Havelock Road. No.40 to 56 Plough Lane and 158 to 166 Havelock Road were completely destroyed and many other houses in these roads were badly damaged. Kingsley Road, Kohat Road, Durnsford Road and Haydons Road were all affected by blast. There were two fatal casualties and twenty-seven injured.

Two more flying bombs hit Wimbledon on Sunday 16th July. The first, which fell a few minutes after midnight, came down between the north booking office of Wimbledon Station and Duff's Depository at the rear of Alexandra Road. One wall and most of the roof of the station booking hall were blown in and the depository, Evans Garage and a number of houses in Alexandra Road were extensively damaged. Cars in the garage caught fire and stacks of furniture that had been salvaged from previous raids burned in the depository. The public library, St. Mark's Hall and Compton Hall were all damaged by the blast, together with a number of shops in Hill Road and on Wimbledon Bridge. A dance had just finished at Wimbledon Town Hall but although the glass roof of the public hall was blown in there were no casualties. However, many people were waiting at the bus stop nearby and of these one was killed and forty-six injured. The second bomb landed on the Common without harm to any buildings but some minor damage was caused in Coombe Lane by a flying bomb that fell in

Merton on the Southern Railway line near Camberley Avenue. There were no incidents on 17th or 18th July but at 10.15 am on the 19th a V-l landed in the vicinity of Warren Farm, causing damage to most of the buildings.

At 3.23 in the morning of Thursday 20th July, No.16 to 26 Wilton Crescent were demolished by a flying bomb and serious damage was caused to all houses from No.2 to 48. On the opposite side of the road, No.3 to 13 were demolished and all houses from 1 to 43 were damaged. The destruction extended to Wilton Grove, Cliveden Road and Kingswood Road and there was glass and roof damage over a wide area. Five people were killed and one of the twenty injured died later in hospital. A week later, in the afternoon of 27th July, houses in these roads were again damaged by a flying bomb that fell at the rear of Springfield House flats in Kingston Road.

Because V-1 flying bombs exploded on or above ground level damage was extensive.

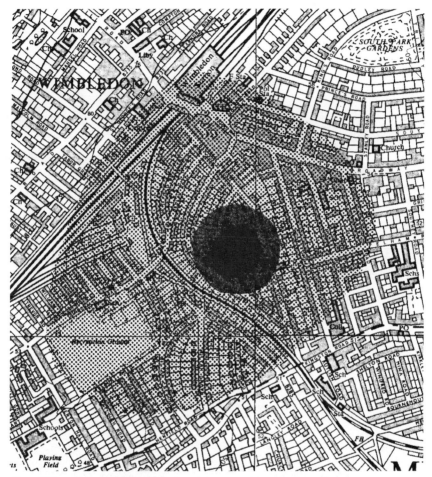

Crown Copyright reserved.

An example of the damage caused by a single V-1 Flying Bomb. The shaded areas show the extent of total destruction (20 houses), buildings seriously damaged (58 houses) and the area of minor damage to roofs, windows, ceilings etc. (580 houses).

The area covered by the above plan is approximately half a square mile and within this area there fell a further six flying bombs, seventy high explosive bombs and fourteen anti-aircraft shells. The positions of these are shown on the main Incident Map.

119

Damage to roofs and windows extended over a wide area.

St. Mathews Church, Durham Road, received a direct hit.

The damage caused by V-1s was so extensive (between three hundred and five hundred houses being damaged by each bomb) that special teams had to be brought in to carry out emergency repairs. In June there had been twenty-four thousand men available in the London area to deal with bomb damage but by the end of July the number had increased to sixty thousand. This rapid increase was achieved in a number of ways. No one with experience in building trades was now called up into the services and labour exchanges throughout the country were directed to send men to London. All London builders who were not engaged on vital work were diverted to first-aid repairs. Factories provided men from their maintenance staffs and retired slaters and tilers helped to repair roofs. Many building workers came over from Ireland and a number of skilled tradesmen were released from the armed forces.

The new buildings of Rutlish School in the Merton area were hit by a flying bomb on 29th July and damage was caused to buildings in Kingston Road, Hartfield Road and Gladstone Road. Six people were injured. The engine of this bomb cut out when it was over South Wimbledon but it pulled out of its dive and skimmed over the rooftops of houses with a sound like an express train, before crashing. Fortunately this was a Saturday and no one was in the school.

A flying bomb that fell on the sixteenth green of the Royal Wimbledon golf course on 31st July caused only minor damage in adjoining roads. Wimbledon Hill was again hit by a flying bomb on 3rd August. It fell slightly lower on the hill than the previous one and caused extensive damage to Wimbledon High School. No.78 Hill Road was destroyed and No.80 and 82 were seriously damaged. The Draxmont Hotel, the flats at the corner of Woodside and a number of other houses were also affected by the blast. Other buildings were damaged in Mansel Road and Raymond Road and there were twenty-two casualties, one of whom died in hospital.

The progress of allied troops in France was now being keenly followed as they approached the areas from which the V-1s were being launched but the air raid warnings continued to sound and the bombs to arrive throughout the month of August. From the direction of Croydon an intensive barrage of gunfire formed a screen through which the bombs had to fly and many were destroyed before they reached Wimbledon.

On 14th August a bomb falling in the Merton area, at Vernon Avenue, caused damage to houses in Pepys Road, Worple Road and Stanton Road. At 9.0 am on 15th August, No.48 to 62 and 49 to 71 Stuart Road, were demolished by a flying bomb and there were twenty-three casualties. The blast damage extended over a very wide area, covering Ashen Grove, Marlborough Road, Arthur Road, Melrose Avenue and the surrounding district. Some strange effects were produced by the blast. Although the complete front of one house was blown away, the picture rail was left spanning from wall to wall with a picture still hanging from it.

Another V-l which fell in the garden of No.120 Home Park Road on 20th August, caused damage to surrounding houses and to houses in Somerset Road, Church Road, Burghley Road and Marryat Road. In the early hours of the morning of 22nd August, Havelock Road was hit by a flying bomb, which demolished houses from No.69 to 75 and 124 to162. Many other houses were seriously damaged and a large water main was burst. In Kingsley Road No.48 to 52 and 53 to 55 were also destroyed and there was severe damage to the remaining houses in this road on both sides. Houses in Kohat Road, Haydons Road, Plough Lane, Gap Road and Cromwell Road also suffered from this bomb. One person was killed and seven people were injured. A Morrison shelter in one of the houses protected the occupants, although part of the bomb was found lying beside it.

At a few minutes past three on the morning of 24th August, a flying bomb landed on tennis courts in Wimbledon Park, damaging houses in Home Park Road, Arthur Road and Melrose Avenue but there was only one casualty. Later that day a bomb fell on the north side of Fishpond Lake in the grounds of Margin House in Marryat Road. Damage was widespread but light.

The last of the V-ls arrived at 3.05 pm on Monday 28th August. It passed over Wimbledon at some height and then, after the engine had stopped, it continued to glide and turning through 180° it headed back into Wimbledon. It crashed among houses in Lambton Road, demolishing No.73 to 79 and damaging all other houses in this road. Houses in Amity Grove, which had previously been damaged, were now destroyed and further havoc was caused in Pendarves Road, Kenwyn Road, Rosevine Road, Pepys Road, Cambridge Road and Durham Road. Two people were killed and twenty-one taken to hospital. After this raid wardens picked over the remains of one of the buildings, which had been the surgery of Dr. Bevan Pritchard. They were concerned in case there should be any dangerous drugs left lying in the rubble. It was thought that the doctor had been out when the bomb fell but he was discovered, uninjured, under the debris. Two sisters, who were in the cellar of another house that was completely destroyed, managed to dig themselves out and then helped to rescue a neighbour. This raid, number 93 in the incident reports, was the last active raid on the borough of Wimbledon. The first of the V-2 rockets fell in Chiswick on 8th September 1944. Although 517 of these rockets landed in Greater London during the following seven months and explosions were frequently heard, none of them landed in Wimbledon.

On 15th September 1944, details were announced in the Wimbledon Borough News of the damage and casualties that had been suffered during the V-1 raids. It was estimated that fifty per cent of all houses in the borough had been damaged and casualties amounted to 648. It was some time before total figures for all the air raids were available and the exact number of houses suffering minor damage has never been accurately determined. The final figures for casualties were 150 killed, 440 seriously injured and 631 requiring first aid treatment. Three hundred and five houses had been destroyed and a further five hundred and five damaged beyond repair. Nine hundred and twenty nine were seriously damaged resulting in over two thousand people being rendered homeless. The reports on minor damage amount to over sixteen thousand but as many of these buildings were damaged several times over a figure of twelve thousand would probably be more accurate.

The Government provided insurance against war damage but this did not compensate for the personal losses that had been involved and it took many years for houses to be rebuilt. Essential repairs to standing buildings had to be completed first and when rebuilding started, smaller houses were given priority. The relative importance and size of any building work had to be assessed before a building licence could be issued. Buildings that were replaced under the insurance scheme had to match as closely as possible those that had been destroyed. This was to prevent any profiteering by owners who might be tempted to build something better than had previously existed. Although this was a fair precaution it meant that improved methods of construction could not be used. Many houses had to be rebuilt exactly as they had been built fifty to a hundred years before. This is why where several houses in a terrace had been destroyed it may now be difficult to see the 'joins'. In some cases, such as when the owner had been killed or there was another reason for not immediately rebuilding, sites would be left empty for a number of years and then sold for an entirely new development. The decorative iron railings and gates that had been such a feature of the Victorian streets were of course never replaced.

Wimbledon had played its part in many ways. At the beginning of the war, when a fund had been started to pay for a Spitfire costing £6,000, it had taken two months to raise the first £2,000 but by the end of the war the borough had contributed £8,000,000 through national savings. In Salute the Soldier Week, which was held at the end of 1944, £705,000 was collected; sufficient to equip six battalions. By the end of the year the danger of air raids had passed and blackout regulations were relaxed. A small amount of street lighting came into use but many of the street lamps had been put out of action by bombing and electrical equipment had deteriorated during the war years. The result was a 'dim out' rather than a 'black out' but at least the journey home was no longer in total darkness.

May 1945 brought the eagerly awaited news of Victory. In the first few days of the month there was confusion because although everyone knew that Hitler was dead and that an armistice had been signed, no official announcement had been made. On 7th May some half-hearted celebrations began but it was not until 3.0pm that an official announcement was made that May 8th was to be a public holiday and celebrations began in earnest.

Some local people went to join the wild rejoicing that was taking place in the West End while others stayed in Wimbledon to organised local events. Huge bonfires were constructed in many of the streets. They burned all night and left the tarmac roads blistered and scorched. Pianos were wheeled out of houses to provide music for dancing in the streets and some parties were visited by a tank that toured South Wimbledon. Children's parties were organised with everyone contributing food from their rations. Punch and Judy shows and magicians appeared as if by magic. At the church hall adjoining Trinity Church in Wimbledon Broadway (now the Polka Theatre) local residents organised a party and put on their own 'Music Hall' performance.

124

One of the many street parties organised for children following VE Day.

The civil defence services and the armed forces took their final salute in a Victory Parade, which assembled at the War Memorial and marched down Wimbledon Hill and past the Town Hall. For most people this was the end of the story but those with friends and relatives serving in the Far East had to postpone their rejoicing until VJ Day. Even after the surrender of Japan it took a long time for the troops to return home and be demobilised. Rationing continued for several years and it took many years to repair or replace all the buildings that had been damaged and destroyed.

But the worst was now over. Another chapter in the long history of Wimbledon was complete.

Victory parade passing the Town Hall

Index of Incidents by Roads

128

129